Automating the World

The Rise of Smart Machines and Robots How automation is reshaping industries and daily life

THOMPSON CARTER

Table of Content

TABLE OF CONTENTS

Introduction

The dawn of **automation** is upon us, and with it comes a wave of profound change that is shaping our industries, our homes, and the very way we live. In recent years, we have witnessed rapid advancements in technologies that were once confined to the realm of science fiction. **Robots, artificial intelligence (AI), machine learning, autonomous systems**, and **smart devices** have all transitioned from being concepts to becoming an integral part of our daily lives. Automation is no longer just a future possibility; it is a present reality that is reshaping the world in profound ways.

This book, "Automating the World: The Rise of Smart Machines and Robots," is a comprehensive exploration of the rapidly expanding field of automation. In these pages, we will delve deep into how automation technologies are not just transforming industries like **manufacturing, healthcare, transportation**, and **finance**, but also redefining societal norms, human relationships with work, and our vision of the future. Through a blend of case studies, real-world examples, and forward-thinking insights, this book aims to offer a clear understanding of how automation is unfolding across various sectors and the immense potential it holds.

Automation, once thought of as something limited to assembly lines and industrial machines, has now spread into every aspect of human life. From **AI-powered chatbots** in customer service to **autonomous drones** delivering packages, the reach of automation is vast. It's no longer confined to complex, high-tech industries but is rapidly expanding into everyday tools, making tasks easier, faster, and more efficient. But automation is not just about convenience or efficiency—it's also about unlocking new possibilities.

As we explore the world of automation, we will also encounter the complexities and challenges it presents. Automation is undeniably a double-edged sword, bringing not only unprecedented advancements but also important ethical, economic, and social questions. How will workers in traditional sectors adapt to new technologies? What happens to jobs that are replaced by robots and AI systems? Can we trust these systems to make decisions for us, and how do we ensure they are fair, transparent, and secure? This book will also address the pressing questions about the future of work, privacy, security, and the implications for our social fabric.

Throughout this book, we will examine:

- The **current state of automation** and the technologies that are driving it forward—how robots and smart machines are already performing tasks that were once human-exclusive and what that means for industries and consumers.

- **Autonomous systems** such as self-driving vehicles and drones, which are revolutionizing transportation, delivery, and logistics, offering a glimpse into the future of mobility.

- **AI** and **machine learning**, which are providing smart solutions to complex problems, improving decision-making, and personalizing experiences in ways that were previously impossible.

- The **role of automation in everyday life**, from smart homes to personal assistants, and how these technologies are designed to improve our quality of life, save time, and increase comfort.

- The **ethical, legal, and social implications** of automation, including its impact on employment, privacy, and the governance of increasingly autonomous systems.

- **Emerging technologies** like quantum computing and blockchain, and their potential to enhance and redefine the future of automation.

This book is not merely a technical exploration of robots or AI; it is a roadmap to understanding how automation is transforming our world. It aims to provide you with both a comprehensive overview of current innovations and a thoughtful look at the societal shifts that automation is driving. Whether you are a technologist, business leader, policymaker, or simply someone curious about the future, this book will give you the insights you need to grasp the monumental changes taking place and understand the far-reaching consequences of automation in our lives.

As we journey into the future of smart machines and robots, we must keep in mind the profound potential for good that these technologies bring—along with the responsibility we bear to shape their evolution in ways that maximize benefit for all. The future is fast approaching, and it is one in which automation will be as integral to our daily existence as the devices and systems we rely on today. The question isn't whether automation will change our world; it's how we will embrace it to create a future that is both innovative and equitable.

Welcome to the future of automation. The journey has already begun.

CHAPTER 1

INTRODUCTION TO AUTOMATION: THE NEW INDUSTRIAL REVOLUTION

Defining Automation and Its Role in Modern Society

Automation refers to the use of technology to perform tasks that would traditionally require human intervention. This can include machines, control systems, and software that work autonomously or with minimal human oversight. In simple terms, automation makes processes faster, more efficient, and often more accurate by replacing manual labor or enhancing human capabilities.

The importance of automation in modern society cannot be overstated. It is a key driver of innovation and economic growth. From self-checkout systems in stores to advanced robotics in manufacturing plants, automation is becoming a fundamental aspect of both everyday life and business operations. It plays a crucial role in reducing costs, increasing productivity, and enabling complex tasks that would otherwise be impossible or too costly for humans to perform.

In essence, automation touches every sector, from healthcare and transportation to entertainment and education. Its benefits are not limited to businesses; consumers also experience the impact in the form of quicker services, personalized experiences, and enhanced convenience.

How Automation is Reshaping Industries and Daily Life

The integration of automation into various industries is reshaping how businesses operate, improving efficiency, and lowering the risk of errors. In manufacturing, automation has enabled the creation of "smart factories" where machines and robots work in sync to optimize production lines. Tasks that once took hours are now completed in minutes, without compromising quality. For example, companies like Tesla and General Motors rely on robots to assemble vehicles with precision, speed, and cost-effectiveness.

In the healthcare sector, automation is revolutionizing patient care. Robotic surgery systems allow for minimally invasive procedures, offering patients quicker recovery times and reducing human error. Additionally, AI-powered diagnostic tools can analyze medical images faster than human doctors, catching diseases like cancer in their earliest stages.

Transportation is another area being transformed by automation. The development of autonomous vehicles, such as self-driving cars, is set to drastically reduce accidents caused by human error, as well as improve traffic flow and reduce fuel consumption. Moreover, automated systems are increasingly used in logistics, with drones delivering packages and robots managing warehouse inventories.

Automation is also impacting daily life in more subtle but profound ways. In homes, smart devices like thermostats, lights, and security systems are becoming commonplace, making daily tasks easier and more energy-efficient. Personal assistants, such as Siri and Alexa, use voice recognition and natural language processing to respond to commands, helping people manage their time and household tasks.

In essence, automation is moving from the industrial domain to the personal sphere, making life more convenient, efficient, and connected. However, while it promises significant improvements, it also raises important questions about the future of jobs and human roles in a world increasingly dominated by smart machines. These challenges will be explored in subsequent chapters.

This chapter sets the stage for the rest of the book, where we will delve deeper into the specific ways automation is reshaping industries, driving innovation, and influencing our daily lives.

4o mini

You said:

• The History of Automation: From the Industrial Revolution to Today • Key milestones in automation history • Evolution of smart machines and robotics

ChatGPT said:

Chapter 2: The History of Automation: From the Industrial Revolution to Today

Key Milestones in Automation History

The history of automation is deeply intertwined with the broader development of industrial technology. It has evolved over centuries, from the early manual methods of production to the highly sophisticated systems of today. Below are key milestones that highlight this transformation:

1. **The Industrial Revolution (Late 18th to Early 19th Century)**

   o The Industrial Revolution marked the first significant shift from manual labor to machine-based production. Innovations such as the steam engine by James Watt and mechanized looms revolutionized industries like textiles, mining, and manufacturing.

   o The introduction of mechanized spinning and weaving machines dramatically increased production efficiency in textile mills. This period set the foundation for future automation, as machines began to take over repetitive and labor-intensive tasks.

2. **The Birth of the Assembly Line (Early 20th Century)**

   o In the early 1900s, Henry Ford introduced the assembly line to automotive manufacturing. This was a pivotal moment in automation history as it allowed mass production of cars at a much lower cost. Ford's system of moving parts along a conveyor belt minimized human labor, increased production speed, and reduced manufacturing costs.

o This was one of the earliest examples of automation in a production environment, where humans and machines worked together in a streamlined process.

3. The Advent of Computers and Early Robots (Mid-20th Century)

o The development of computers in the 1940s and 1950s brought about the first stages of digital automation. Machines were able to follow instructions or programs to perform tasks autonomously, laying the groundwork for future advancements in smart automation.

o In the 1960s, the first industrial robots, such as Unimate, were introduced. These robotic arms were used for tasks such as welding and material handling in car manufacturing, marking the start of robotics in factories.

4. The Rise of Computer-Aided Design (CAD) and Computer Numerical Control (CNC) (1970s-1980s)

o The 1970s saw the introduction of Computer-Aided Design (CAD), allowing engineers to design products digitally. This innovation was coupled with Computer Numerical Control

17

(CNC) machines, which allowed automated manufacturing processes to be controlled via computers.

o These innovations increased precision in manufacturing and enabled rapid prototyping and more complex designs to be created and produced more efficiently.

5. **The Birth of Personal Computers and the Internet (1980s-1990s)**

   o The personal computer revolution in the 1980s, followed by the rise of the internet in the 1990s, allowed for global connectivity and data sharing. Businesses could now control processes remotely, monitor production in real-time, and even automate entire supply chains.

   o As the internet became widespread, cloud computing emerged, giving rise to remote automation tools, and creating the foundation for the Internet of Things (IoT), where devices could connect and operate autonomously.

6. **The Introduction of Collaborative Robots (2010s)**

   o In the 2010s, the concept of collaborative robots (cobots) was introduced, designed to work alongside humans rather than replace them. These robots could assist in manufacturing by performing repetitive or dangerous tasks, while humans handled more complex or intricate operations.

- o Cobots marked a significant evolution in the relationship between humans and robots, making automation more accessible to small and medium-sized businesses.

Evolution of Smart Machines and Robotics

The evolution of smart machines and robotics is one of the most fascinating aspects of modern automation. What started as simple machines designed to perform repetitive tasks has transformed into highly intelligent systems capable of learning, decision-making, and interacting with their environment.

1. **Early Robotics and Automation**
    - o Early robots were primarily designed for industrial applications. They were large, heavy machines that required specialized skills to operate. These robots performed highly repetitive tasks like welding, assembly, and painting in automotive plants.
    - o Although they were efficient, these early robots lacked flexibility and required human programming for each task. They could not adapt

to new tasks or environments without significant intervention.

2. The Rise of Artificial Intelligence (AI)

- o In the 21st century, the integration of AI with robotics ushered in a new era of smart machines. AI allows robots to make decisions, learn from experience, and adapt to their surroundings. This is a significant leap forward from earlier robots, which could only execute pre-programmed tasks.

- o Smart machines now use AI and machine learning algorithms to optimize their functions. For example, AI-powered robots can navigate complex environments (like a robot vacuum navigating a home) by learning from past experiences and making real-time decisions.

3. Robotics in New Industries

- o Robotics has moved beyond manufacturing into new industries such as healthcare, agriculture, and logistics. Robots are now used in surgeries, where they assist or even perform complex procedures with more precision than human surgeons. In agriculture, drones and automated tractors are changing the way crops are planted, monitored, and harvested.

- o The rise of autonomous vehicles, including self-driving cars and drones, represents another breakthrough. These machines use a combination of sensors, AI, and data processing to navigate and make decisions independently, radically changing the transportation industry.

4. The Integration of the Internet of Things (IoT)

- o IoT plays a vital role in the development of smart machines. By connecting machines and devices to the internet, manufacturers and businesses can automate tasks on a larger scale. This connectivity allows machines to communicate with each other, share data, and work in concert to optimize processes.

- o For example, in smart factories, machines can autonomously order parts, repair themselves, and even shut down if something goes wrong, all through interconnected IoT systems.

5. The Future of Robotics and Smart Machines

- o As robotics and smart machines continue to evolve, they are becoming more autonomous, intelligent, and capable of handling a broader range of tasks. We are seeing robots not only in factories but also in our homes, schools, hospitals, and even space.

- o The future of automation is expected to see even more sophisticated robots that can perform complex tasks with minimal human input. These

21

robots will have advanced sensory capabilities, enhanced AI algorithms, and improved physical dexterity, making them highly effective in industries like healthcare, construction, and logistics.

This chapter gives readers a comprehensive overview of the historical progression of automation and its role in shaping modern society. From the early days of mechanized production to the rise of AI-powered robots, it establishes the foundation for understanding how automation is impacting industries and will continue to do so in the future.

CHAPTER 3

UNDERSTANDING SMART MACHINES: WHAT MAKES THEM 'SMART'

Defining Smart Machines and Their Capabilities

Smart machines are systems designed to perform tasks autonomously, often with minimal human intervention, by using advanced technologies like artificial intelligence (AI), machine learning, sensors, and data processing. Unlike traditional machines that require human input or pre-programmed instructions for every action, smart machines are capable of adapting to new situations, making decisions, and optimizing their functions in real-time.

The term "smart" in smart machines refers to the ability of these devices to make intelligent decisions based on the data they receive from their environment, learn from those inputs, and improve their operations over time. These machines can analyze data, detect patterns, and perform complex actions with an increasing level of sophistication. Some key capabilities of smart machines include:

1. **Autonomy**: Smart machines can perform tasks without constant supervision or manual control. For example, a self-driving car can navigate and adjust to traffic conditions without needing a human driver.

2. **Adaptability**: They can adjust their behavior based on changing environments or new data. This allows them to function in dynamic or unpredictable conditions, such as industrial robots learning to handle various types of products on a factory floor.

3. **Real-time Decision-Making**: These machines can make decisions instantly based on real-time inputs, which is especially critical in applications like autonomous vehicles or robotic surgery.

4. **Learning and Improvement**: Through AI and machine learning, smart machines improve their performance over time by learning from experiences and past data. A smart vacuum cleaner, for instance, learns the layout of a room and optimizes its cleaning path for better efficiency.

5. **Interaction**: Some smart machines can communicate with other machines, systems, or humans. For example, IoT-enabled devices like smart thermostats or voice assistants can interact

with users and other connected devices to offer more personalized services.

Basic Principles of How Smart Machines Work (AI, Sensors, etc.)

To understand how smart machines work, it's important to look at the fundamental technologies that drive their capabilities. These include artificial intelligence (AI), machine learning, sensors, and data processing. Here's a breakdown of each:

1. **Artificial Intelligence (AI)**
   - AI enables machines to simulate human intelligence, allowing them to make decisions, solve problems, and even recognize patterns. At its core, AI mimics how humans think, process information, and learn from experiences.
   - **Machine Learning (ML)** is a subset of AI where machines are trained to recognize patterns and make decisions based on data. For instance, AI in self-driving cars uses machine learning to learn from road conditions, traffic patterns, and the behavior of other drivers to make real-time driving decisions.
   - **Deep Learning**, a subset of machine learning, uses neural networks that are inspired by the

25

human brain. This allows smart machines to perform tasks like image recognition, speech recognition, and language translation with remarkable accuracy.

2. **Sensors**

   o Sensors play a crucial role in how smart machines perceive and interact with their environment. These devices collect data from the world around them, which is then processed and used by AI to make decisions or trigger actions.

   o **Types of Sensors**:

      ▪ **Proximity sensors**: Used in robots to detect the presence of objects or obstacles.

      ▪ **Vision sensors (cameras)**: Used in machines like drones or autonomous vehicles for object recognition and navigation.

      ▪ **Temperature sensors**: Found in smart thermostats, these sensors detect temperature changes to optimize heating or cooling in homes.

      ▪ **Pressure sensors**: Used in industries like manufacturing to monitor the weight and pressure of materials.

3. **Data Processing and Analytics**

○ Once sensors collect data, the next step is processing that data in real time. This is where the power of AI and machine learning comes in. Data is often analyzed to identify trends, make predictions, or adjust the machine's behavior accordingly.

○ **Big Data Analytics** is used in smart machines to handle vast amounts of data. For example, in manufacturing, sensors in smart factories continuously send data about machine performance, which is then analyzed to predict when a machine will need maintenance, reducing downtime and improving efficiency.

4. **Connectivity and IoT (Internet of Things)**

○ Many smart machines are interconnected through IoT, allowing them to share data and collaborate to complete tasks more efficiently. For example, in a smart home, a security camera, door lock, and motion sensor might all work together to detect and respond to unusual activity.

○ **Edge Computing** plays a key role here, where data is processed closer to the source (at the "edge") rather than being sent to a centralized server. This minimizes delays, enabling faster decision-making for time-sensitive applications, such as autonomous vehicles or industrial robots.

27

5. Human-Machine Interaction

- One of the fascinating aspects of smart machines is their ability to interact with humans through voice commands, touch, or visual recognition. Virtual assistants like Amazon's Alexa, Google Assistant, or Apple's Siri, for instance, allow users to control various devices, ask questions, or perform tasks by simply speaking to them.

- **Natural Language Processing (NLP)** is the technology that enables machines to understand and respond to human language. This allows smart machines to engage in conversations, answer queries, and even assist in more complex tasks, such as scheduling appointments or controlling home automation systems.

6. Robotics and Actuators

- In robotics, actuators serve as the muscles of the robot, enabling movement and physical interaction with the environment. These actuators, combined with AI and sensors, allow robots to perform tasks like picking up objects, assembling products, or even interacting with humans in a meaningful way.

- For example, collaborative robots (cobots) are designed to work alongside human operators in factories. They use AI to understand the human

28

worker's actions and adapt their behavior in real time, ensuring efficiency while maintaining safety.

This chapter provides a detailed understanding of what makes machines "smart" and the key technologies that enable them to function autonomously. The integration of AI, sensors, machine learning, and real-time data processing allows these machines to perform tasks that once seemed impossible. As smart machines continue to evolve, they will reshape not only industries but also our day-to-day lives.

CHAPTER 4

HOW ROBOTS ARE CHANGING THE WORKFORCE

Role of Robots in Manufacturing and Service Industries

Robots are no longer confined to science fiction or industrial workshops; they have become integral to various industries, particularly in manufacturing and service sectors. Their role in the workforce has evolved significantly, with robots now performing a wide range of tasks that were once done by humans. Their ability to enhance efficiency, reduce costs, and improve safety is transforming industries around the world.

1. **Manufacturing Industry**
   o **Automation of Repetitive Tasks**: In manufacturing, robots are used to perform repetitive tasks that would otherwise be labor-intensive and time-consuming. These tasks include assembly line work, welding, painting, and packaging. Robots excel in these areas because they can work continuously without fatigue, ensuring consistent product quality.

30

- o **Increased Precision and Quality Control**: Robots are highly accurate and precise, which is crucial in manufacturing sectors like electronics, automotive, and aerospace. For example, robotic arms are used in car production to weld parts with high precision, reducing human error and improving overall vehicle safety.

2. **Service Industry**

   - o **Customer Service**: Robots are also making their mark in the service industry, particularly in customer-facing roles. Self-service kiosks, robotic receptionists, and automated check-in systems are increasingly being adopted in sectors like hospitality, retail, and airports. These robots enhance the customer experience by reducing wait times and allowing for 24/7 service.

   - o **Healthcare and Elderly Care**: Robots are playing an essential role in healthcare, assisting with patient care, diagnostics, and surgeries. For example, robots help lift patients, deliver medications, or monitor health data. In elderly care, robots are helping with daily activities, reminding patients to take their medication, or even offering companionship, thus improving quality of life for the elderly and reducing the strain on human caregivers.

31

3. Logistics and Warehousing

- In logistics and supply chain management, robots are enhancing the speed and efficiency of order fulfillment, sorting, and delivery. Automated Guided Vehicles (AGVs) are used in warehouses to transport goods across large facilities, while robotic arms assist with picking and packing orders. Companies like Amazon have already implemented robots in their warehouses to help sort packages, increasing productivity and reducing operational costs.

Real-World Examples of Robots Replacing or Assisting Humans

1. Automotive Manufacturing – Tesla and General Motors

- Tesla's manufacturing plants use robots extensively in the assembly process. From robotic arms performing tasks such as welding and painting to fully automated lines for assembly and inspection, robots help streamline operations. These robots increase production speed, reduce the chance of human error, and maintain a high level of consistency across all vehicles produced.
- General Motors has also integrated robots into their assembly lines. For example, robotic arms

32

perform precision welding and assembly of car parts, which are crucial for the strength and safety of the vehicle. This has allowed GM to scale production and maintain tight quality control while reducing labor costs.

2. **Healthcare – Robotic Surgery and Assistive Robots**

   o Robotic systems like **da Vinci Surgical System** have revolutionized the healthcare industry by assisting surgeons in performing minimally invasive surgeries with higher precision. These systems provide detailed visualizations and can make small, precise incisions, leading to quicker recovery times for patients and reducing the risk of complications.

   o In elderly care, robots like **Paro**, a therapeutic robot designed to look like a baby seal, help reduce stress and loneliness in elderly patients, particularly those suffering from conditions like dementia. These robots provide comfort, assist with physical tasks, and interact with patients, improving their emotional well-being.

3. **Retail – Amazon's Automated Warehouses**

   o Amazon has implemented robots to enhance the efficiency of its fulfillment centers. Robots like **Kiva Systems** (now Amazon Robotics) are used

33

to transport shelves of goods to human pickers. This automation has dramatically sped up the order fulfillment process, allowing Amazon to handle millions of orders daily while reducing human labor in the process.

o In grocery stores, robots like **Marty** in Giant Eagle and **Tally** in Walmart use sensors and cameras to scan shelves, detect out-of-stock items, and ensure that items are properly stocked and displayed. These robots assist employees by taking over mundane tasks, allowing them to focus on more critical responsibilities, like helping customers.

4. **Agriculture – John Deere's Autonomous Tractors**

o In agriculture, robots are transforming how farms operate. John Deere's **autonomous tractors** are capable of planting, watering, and harvesting crops without the need for a human operator. These tractors use GPS technology, sensors, and AI to navigate fields, optimize planting patterns, and monitor soil conditions. This automation is making farming more efficient, sustainable, and cost-effective.

o Robots like **Octinion's Rubion** are designed to pick strawberries in fields. These robots are equipped with advanced vision systems to detect

34

ripe fruit and delicate handling mechanisms to pick strawberries without damaging them. This helps address labor shortages and increases the speed of harvesting.

5. **Hospitality – Robots in Hotels**

   o Hotels are increasingly using robots to automate certain aspects of their operations. For example, **Connie**, a robot concierge developed by Hilton, interacts with guests and provides information about the hotel's amenities, local attractions, and room service options. By handling routine inquiries, Connie frees up hotel staff to focus on more personalized guest services.

   o In Japan, robots like **Pepper** are used as hotel receptionists, greeting guests and checking them in. This helps hotels save on human labor and ensures that guests have a modern, tech-savvy experience during their stay.

6. **Transportation – Autonomous Delivery Robots**

   o In urban areas, **autonomous delivery robots** are making waves by providing on-demand deliveries directly to consumers. For instance, companies like **Starship Technologies** use small, autonomous robots to deliver food and packages within a short radius. These robots navigate sidewalks, avoid obstacles, and use AI to

35

determine the fastest routes, offering a more efficient and cost-effective delivery solution compared to traditional methods.

o **Autonomous trucks** are being tested by companies like **Waymo** and **Tesla**. These trucks can transport goods across long distances without human drivers, improving delivery efficiency and safety. As these technologies develop, the trucking industry may experience a major shift toward automation.

This chapter explores how robots are not only transforming the workforce but also creating new opportunities in various sectors. From improving productivity and efficiency to enhancing safety and quality of life, robots are becoming vital collaborators in industries like manufacturing, healthcare, logistics, and retail. These real-world examples highlight how robots are replacing or assisting humans, and their role is expected to continue expanding as technology progresses.

CHAPTER 5

AI AND MACHINE LEARNING IN AUTOMATION

Understanding the Relationship Between AI and Automation

Artificial Intelligence (AI) and automation are deeply interconnected, with AI serving as the driving force behind many advanced automation systems. While automation refers to the use of technology to perform tasks without human intervention, AI adds a layer of intelligence, enabling machines to make decisions, learn from experience, and adapt to changing environments.

AI in Automation involves using algorithms and data to allow machines to perform tasks that typically require human intelligence. These tasks include decision-making, problem-solving, pattern recognition, and even understanding natural language. By integrating AI into automation systems, machines not only perform repetitive tasks but can also handle complex, dynamic situations where human-like reasoning is required.

Machine Learning (ML), a subset of AI, is particularly vital in automation. ML allows machines to learn from data, identify patterns, and improve their performance over time. This makes them adaptable to new scenarios without requiring explicit programming for every task. For example, a robot vacuum cleaner can learn the layout of a room and optimize its cleaning path without human intervention.

The relationship between AI and automation is symbiotic:

- **AI** makes machines smarter by enabling them to interpret data and make decisions.
- **Automation** makes processes more efficient by handling repetitive or dangerous tasks, and AI helps automate more complex, decision-based processes.

Real-Life Applications Like Self-Driving Cars, Chatbots, etc.

The integration of AI and automation is already transforming many industries. Here are some real-world applications that demonstrate how this synergy is changing the way we live and work:

1. **Self-Driving Cars**
   - **AI in Self-Driving Cars**: Self-driving cars, like those developed by Tesla, Waymo, and other

companies, use AI to navigate roads, make decisions, and avoid obstacles. These vehicles rely on a variety of AI technologies, including computer vision, natural language processing, and machine learning.

○ **How it Works**: The car's AI system collects data from sensors, cameras, and LIDAR (Light Detection and Ranging) systems. This data is processed in real-time to identify road signs, pedestrians, traffic signals, and other vehicles. Based on this information, the AI system makes decisions about steering, braking, and acceleration.

○ **The Role of Machine Learning**: Over time, self-driving cars use machine learning to improve their performance. They can adapt to new driving conditions, learn from previous experiences, and even improve their ability to predict and react to other drivers' behaviors.

2. **Chatbots and Virtual Assistants**

○ **AI in Customer Service**: Chatbots, like those used by companies such as Bank of America (Erica) or Amazon (Alexa), use AI and natural language processing (NLP) to understand and respond to customer inquiries. These bots can handle a wide range of tasks, from answering basic questions to processing transactions and troubleshooting issues.

- o **How it Works**: Chatbots rely on machine learning algorithms that analyze conversations and continuously improve their understanding of human language. NLP helps them process spoken or written language, while deep learning enables the bots to improve responses over time.

- o **Benefits**: Chatbots provide instant support 24/7, reducing the need for human agents and enhancing customer satisfaction. They are particularly useful for handling high volumes of routine inquiries, allowing human agents to focus on more complex tasks.

3. **Predictive Maintenance in Manufacturing**

- o **AI in Manufacturing**: In manufacturing, AI-powered systems are used to predict equipment failures before they occur. Sensors collect data from machines, and AI algorithms analyze this data to identify patterns that could indicate wear and tear or potential malfunctions.

- o **How it Works**: Predictive maintenance systems use machine learning models to forecast when equipment is likely to fail, enabling maintenance teams to take proactive action. This prevents costly downtime and extends the lifespan of machinery.

- o **Real-World Example**: General Electric (GE) uses AI-powered predictive maintenance in its aircraft engines. By analyzing data from sensors embedded in the engines, GE can predict potential failures and perform maintenance before problems arise, reducing repair costs and improving flight safety.

4. **AI in Healthcare: Diagnosing Diseases**

- o **AI in Diagnostics**: AI has become a crucial tool in healthcare, especially for diagnosing diseases like cancer, heart conditions, and neurological disorders. Machine learning algorithms analyze medical images such as X-rays, CT scans, and MRIs to detect abnormalities that might be missed by human doctors.

- o **How it Works**: AI algorithms are trained on vast amounts of medical data, allowing them to learn how to identify patterns in medical images that are associated with specific conditions. These systems improve their accuracy over time as they process more data.

- o **Real-World Example**: IBM's Watson Health is one example of AI being used to diagnose diseases. Watson has analyzed thousands of medical research papers and case studies, allowing it to assist doctors in diagnosing diseases and recommending personalized treatment plans.

5. **Robotic Process Automation (RPA)**

   o **AI in Business Operations**: Robotic Process Automation (RPA) is used to automate repetitive tasks in industries like banking, insurance, and human resources. AI-enhanced RPA systems can handle more complex tasks than traditional automation systems.

   o **How it Works**: RPA systems automate routine tasks such as data entry, processing transactions, and customer queries. AI is added to enable RPA to handle tasks that require decision-making, such as identifying patterns in data or interpreting unstructured documents (e.g., emails or contracts).

   o **Real-World Example**: In the financial sector, companies like UiPath are using AI-powered RPA to automate everything from processing loans to detecting fraud. These systems use machine learning to continuously improve their accuracy and efficiency.

6. **Smart Manufacturing and Supply Chain Management**

42

- o **AI in Supply Chains**: AI is being used to optimize supply chain operations, from demand forecasting to inventory management. Machine learning models can predict fluctuations in demand and adjust stock levels accordingly, reducing waste and improving efficiency.
- o **How it Works**: AI systems analyze vast amounts of historical and real-time data, including consumer behavior, market trends, and production schedules. This allows businesses to forecast demand more accurately and automate restocking processes.
- o **Real-World Example**: Walmart uses AI to optimize its inventory management. By analyzing data from its supply chain, the system predicts product demand and ensures that stock levels are adjusted accordingly, reducing stockouts and overstock situations.

In this chapter, we've explored how AI and machine learning are reshaping automation across various industries, providing real-world examples of their application in self-driving cars, chatbots, manufacturing, healthcare, and more. The relationship between AI and automation is not just about machines performing tasks; it's about machines becoming smarter, learning from data, and continuously improving their ability to make decisions and adapt to new situations. As AI continues to evolve, its role in automation will only expand, driving innovation and transforming industries.

CHAPTER 6

THE RISE OF AUTONOMOUS VEHICLES: REVOLUTIONIZING TRANSPORTATION

How Autonomous Vehicles Work

Autonomous vehicles (AVs), often referred to as self-driving cars, represent one of the most exciting applications of AI, machine learning, and automation. These vehicles are designed to operate without human input, using a combination of sensors, cameras, radar, and artificial intelligence (AI) to navigate roads, understand traffic conditions, and make decisions in real-time.

The primary components of autonomous vehicles that enable them to drive themselves include:

1. **Sensors and Cameras**:
    - **LIDAR (Light Detection and Ranging)**: LIDAR uses laser beams to scan the environment and create high-definition 3D maps of the vehicle's surroundings. It helps detect objects,

people, and other vehicles, even in low-light conditions.

o **Radar**: Radar sensors detect objects by sending out radio waves and measuring the reflection. These are particularly useful in bad weather conditions like rain or fog, where visual sensors might struggle.

o **Cameras**: Multiple high-definition cameras around the vehicle provide a 360-degree view. They are used to detect traffic signs, lane markings, pedestrians, and other vehicles.

2. **AI and Machine Learning**:

o The data from sensors and cameras is processed by AI algorithms that interpret the vehicle's surroundings. Machine learning allows the vehicle to make decisions based on past experiences, recognize patterns, and predict what will happen next.

o For example, when an autonomous car approaches an intersection, the AI evaluates the likelihood of pedestrians crossing, the speed of other vehicles, and the traffic lights to decide whether to stop or go.

3. **Control Systems**:

o These systems receive instructions from the AI algorithms and act on them to control the vehicle's movements. They are responsible for steering, accelerating, and braking, ensuring the vehicle follows the road, keeps a safe distance from other cars, and responds to obstacles in real time.

4. **Connectivity**:

   o   Autonomous vehicles often rely on vehicle-to-vehicle (V2V) and vehicle-to-infrastructure (V2I) communication systems to share information about road conditions, traffic, and potential hazards. This connectivity enhances the vehicle's ability to make informed decisions and react to changes in the environment.

The combination of these components enables an autonomous vehicle to perform tasks that would normally require human input, such as driving, stopping at traffic lights, merging into traffic, and avoiding obstacles.

Case Studies: Tesla, Waymo, and More

1. **Tesla's Autopilot and Full Self-Driving (FSD)**

   o   **Tesla's Vision**: Tesla has been a pioneer in bringing autonomous driving technology to the mass market. The company's **Autopilot** system, while not fully autonomous, offers features such as adaptive cruise control, lane centering, and

47

automated lane changes. Tesla's **Full Self-Driving (FSD)** package promises even more advanced capabilities, including automatic navigation on highways, self-parking, and the ability to summon the car from a parking spot.

- o **How it Works**: Tesla vehicles use a combination of **cameras, radar, and ultrasonic sensors** to detect the environment around the car. Unlike other autonomous vehicle manufacturers, Tesla relies heavily on cameras rather than LIDAR for its vision. The data from these sensors is processed by Tesla's AI software, which constantly updates itself through over-the-air software updates, improving the car's performance.

- o **Challenges and Controversies**: Despite Tesla's innovations, the company's autonomous driving technology has faced challenges and controversies. Some incidents involving Tesla vehicles in autopilot mode have raised questions about the reliability of the technology. Tesla's approach to self-driving is also different from that of other companies, relying more on vision-based systems and less on LIDAR, which some experts believe provides more accurate data.

o **Real-World Impact**: Tesla's vehicles with Autopilot and FSD features represent the closest we have to semi-autonomous cars available for consumers today. While these systems don't yet replace human drivers entirely, they're a significant step forward, offering enhanced safety and convenience.

2. **Waymo: The Leader in Full Autonomy**

o **Waymo's Approach**: Waymo, a subsidiary of Alphabet (Google's parent company), is one of the leaders in the race to develop fully autonomous vehicles. Waymo's goal is to develop cars that can drive without any human intervention in all conditions, and they have made significant progress towards this goal.

o **How it Works**: Waymo vehicles are equipped with a full suite of sensors, including **LIDAR, radar, and cameras**. The combination of these technologies allows Waymo cars to map the environment in high resolution, detect objects at long distances, and make safe driving decisions.

o **Real-World Testing**: Waymo has been conducting real-world testing of its autonomous vehicles in cities like Phoenix, Arizona, where the company has a public robotaxi service. The service allows passengers to hail an autonomous vehicle through an app, which takes them to their destination without a human driver. Waymo's cars are tested in diverse environments, from urban areas with dense traffic to rural roads, ensuring the system can adapt to various driving conditions.

o **Challenges**: Despite Waymo's success, fully autonomous vehicles still face challenges. For example, while the system performs exceptionally well in controlled environments, it can struggle in complex urban areas with unpredictable human behavior. Legal and regulatory hurdles also remain a significant challenge to the widespread deployment of autonomous vehicles.

3. **Cruise (General Motors)**

o **Cruise's Vision**: Cruise, owned by General Motors (GM), is another key player in the autonomous vehicle race. Cruise is developing fully autonomous vehicles without steering wheels or pedals, aiming for a driverless future.

o **How it Works**: Similar to Waymo, Cruise uses **LIDAR, radar, and cameras** to create a 360-degree view of the vehicle's surroundings. These sensors feed data to Cruise's AI algorithms, which interpret the environment and make driving decisions.

o **Real-World Testing**: Cruise has been testing its autonomous vehicles in San Francisco, with plans to expand to other cities. The company's goal is to offer ride-hailing services similar to Waymo's robotaxi service, but with an even more ambitious goal of eliminating human drivers entirely.

o **Challenges**: As with other companies, Cruise faces significant regulatory and safety concerns. Autonomous vehicles need to meet strict safety standards before they can be deployed at scale. Cruise is working closely with regulators to ensure that its vehicles meet safety requirements.

4. **Other Players in the Autonomous Vehicle Market**

o **Aurora**: Aurora is working on autonomous technology for several industries, including freight transportation and passenger vehicles. Aurora's trucks, designed for the freight industry, are being tested in real-world scenarios to transport goods autonomously.

o **Uber ATG (Advanced Technologies Group)**: Uber has been working on developing self-driving cars for its ride-hailing service. While the company has faced setbacks, including a fatal accident in 2018, it continues to invest in autonomous vehicle technology.

Autonomous vehicles are set to revolutionize transportation by reducing accidents, lowering transportation costs, and improving efficiency. Companies like **Tesla**, **Waymo**, and **Cruise** are at the forefront of this innovation, each taking different approaches to achieving fully autonomous driving. While there are still challenges to overcome, including regulatory issues, safety concerns, and technical hurdles, the potential for autonomous vehicles to change how we travel and interact with the world is immense. As technology continues to evolve, the future of transportation may look very different than it does today.

CHAPTER 7

SMART HOMES: THE INTEGRATION OF AUTOMATION INTO DAILY LIFE

The Rise of IoT and Smart Home Devices

The concept of a "smart home" is no longer a futuristic dream; it has become a reality in many households around the world. At the heart of this transformation is the **Internet of Things (IoT)**, a network of interconnected devices that communicate and work together to enhance convenience, security, energy efficiency, and entertainment. These smart devices are powered by automation, AI, and advanced sensors, allowing them to learn from user behavior and make decisions based on real-time data.

The rise of IoT has led to an explosion of smart home devices that allow homeowners to control everything from lighting and temperature to security and entertainment systems—often through voice commands or smartphone apps. With advancements in wireless communication and data processing, smart home devices can now integrate seamlessly into our daily lives, making our homes more intelligent, responsive, and adaptable.

Some key drivers behind the growth of smart homes and IoT include:

1. **Increased Connectivity**: The advent of high-speed internet and 5G networks has enabled devices to communicate faster and more reliably.
2. **Affordability**: As the technology has matured, the cost of smart devices has dropped, making them accessible to a broader market.
3. **Energy Efficiency**: Smart home devices help homeowners optimize energy use, reducing utility costs and minimizing their environmental footprint.
4. **User Convenience**: With voice assistants, smartphones, and automation, smart homes provide a level of convenience and personalization that was previously impossible.

Examples: Amazon Alexa, Google Home, Smart Thermostats

Smart homes are primarily built around devices that provide seamless control, enhance user comfort, and offer intelligent automation. Here are some real-world examples of popular smart home devices:

1. **Amazon Alexa**

   o **Overview**: Amazon Alexa is a voice-controlled virtual assistant that powers a variety of smart devices, including the Amazon Echo speaker. Alexa can perform a wide range of tasks, such as playing music, setting alarms, controlling smart home devices, providing weather updates, and even making shopping lists.

   o **How It Works**: Alexa uses **Natural Language Processing (NLP)** and **machine learning** to understand voice commands and respond accordingly. Over time, Alexa learns a user's preferences, routines, and habits, offering personalized recommendations and automating tasks based on voice interactions.

   o **Real-World Example**: With Amazon Alexa, you can control lights, security cameras, and thermostats using only your voice. For example, you could say, "Alexa, dim the lights" or "Alexa, lock the front door," and Alexa will perform those actions through connected devices, such as smart bulbs or locks.

   o **Alexa Routines**: Alexa can also be programmed with "Routines" to automate everyday tasks. For instance, a user can set a routine where, in the morning, Alexa turns on the lights, plays a favorite song, and provides a weather forecast, all at the same time.

2. **Google Home**

   o **Overview**: Google Home is another leading smart home assistant, powered by **Google Assistant**. It performs similar functions to Amazon Alexa, including controlling smart devices, answering questions, and providing information like traffic updates or news.

   o **How It Works**: Google Home integrates with Google's powerful AI and search capabilities to offer a more refined experience when it comes to knowledge-based tasks. Google Assistant uses voice recognition to understand commands and provide intelligent responses.

   o **Real-World Example**: With Google Home, users can issue commands like, "Hey Google, set the thermostat to 72 degrees," or "Hey Google, play my workout playlist." Google Home can also manage smart home devices, such as lights, security cameras, and appliances, making it easy to adjust settings from anywhere in the house.

   o **Integration with Other Devices**: Google Home works with a wide variety of smart home products, from thermostats like **Nest** to security cameras like **Nest Cam**, providing a comprehensive, easy-to-use platform for home automation.

3. **Smart Thermostats (e.g., Nest, Ecobee)**

   o **Overview**: Smart thermostats are one of the most popular and energy-efficient smart home devices. These devices learn the homeowner's behavior and adjust the temperature accordingly, optimizing energy use and providing greater control over heating and cooling systems.

   o **How They Work**: Smart thermostats use **sensors** and **Wi-Fi connectivity** to learn and adapt to user habits. For example, if you tend to adjust the temperature at certain times of the day or when you leave the house, the thermostat will remember these preferences and automate those actions in the future.

   o **Real-World Example**: **Nest Thermostat**, now owned by Google, is one of the best-known smart thermostats. It can be controlled remotely via a smartphone app, and it adjusts the temperature automatically when you leave or return home. Over time, the system learns your patterns, adjusting to optimize energy use and save on utility bills.

   o **Ecobee** is another smart thermostat that integrates with Amazon Alexa and Google

Assistant. In addition to standard temperature controls, Ecobee has built-in sensors to detect occupancy in different rooms, ensuring that the right temperature is maintained in areas that are actually in use, further improving energy efficiency.

4. **Smart Lighting (e.g., Philips Hue, LIFX)**

   o **Overview**: Smart lighting systems like **Philips Hue** and **LIFX** offer advanced control over home lighting. These systems allow users to control the brightness, color, and on/off status of their lights remotely via an app or voice assistant.

   o **How It Works**: Smart lights connect to your home Wi-Fi or Bluetooth network and can be controlled through voice commands or a smartphone app. They can also be set to operate automatically based on schedules or triggered by certain events, such as motion or time of day.

   o **Real-World Example**: **Philips Hue** smart bulbs allow users to create personalized lighting scenes, adjust the ambiance for different activities (like reading or watching movies), and even sync lights with music or movies for an immersive experience. They can be controlled using Amazon Alexa, Google Assistant, or through the Philips Hue app.

5. **Smart Security Systems (e.g., Ring, Arlo)**

- **Overview**: Smart home security systems have become increasingly popular for ensuring home safety and peace of mind. Devices like **Ring Video Doorbells** and **Arlo security cameras** offer remote monitoring and real-time alerts, allowing homeowners to keep an eye on their property from anywhere.

- **How They Work**: These systems use **motion detection sensors** and **cameras** to monitor the surroundings. When an event is detected (e.g., motion at the door or unusual activity in the yard), the system sends an alert to the homeowner's phone. The user can then view the live video feed, speak through the intercom, or take action.

- **Real-World Example**: **Ring**'s video doorbells allow users to see who's at the door, speak to visitors remotely, and even lock or unlock doors from a distance. Similarly, **Arlo** cameras provide a live video feed and can be programmed to send alerts when motion is detected, ensuring homeowners stay connected to their property at all times.

59

Smart homes, powered by IoT and automation, are transforming the way we interact with our living spaces. Devices like **Amazon Alexa**, **Google Home**, and **smart thermostats** provide convenience, comfort, and energy efficiency, while smart security systems keep homes safer. As technology continues to evolve, the integration of smart devices will only become more seamless, offering greater control and intelligence over our homes. Whether it's adjusting the temperature, controlling the lights, or ensuring security, smart homes are redefining the meaning of a connected lifestyle.

CHAPTER 8

ROBOTS IN HEALTHCARE: CHANGING MEDICINE AND PATIENT CARE

How Robots Are Being Used in Surgery, Elderly Care, and Diagnostics

Robots are making profound changes in healthcare by improving the precision of surgeries, enhancing patient care, and helping doctors diagnose diseases with greater accuracy. These innovations are not just limited to improving surgical outcomes but also play an integral role in the care of the elderly and in advancing diagnostic capabilities.

1. **Robotic Surgery**
   - **Minimally Invasive Surgery**: Robotic surgery systems are transforming the way surgeries are performed. These robots allow for minimally invasive procedures where the surgeon makes small incisions rather than large ones. The robotic arms are equipped with specialized instruments, and through these small incisions, the robot can perform complex surgeries with high precision.

o **How It Works**: The surgeon controls the robotic system via a console that translates their hand movements into highly precise robotic actions. The robotic system provides a 3D, high-definition view of the surgical area, which helps the surgeon perform the surgery with greater accuracy and less strain.

o **Benefits**: This technology reduces blood loss, speeds up recovery times, lowers the risk of infection, and shortens hospital stays. It also allows for more complex surgeries that might otherwise require larger incisions or more extensive human effort.

2. **Robotic Assistance in Elderly Care**

o **Robotic Companions**: As the global population ages, robots are increasingly being used to assist with the care of the elderly. Robots like **Paro**, a therapeutic robot designed to resemble a baby seal, help alleviate loneliness and stress among elderly patients, particularly those with dementia. These robots offer comfort, companionship, and cognitive stimulation.

o **Assistive Robots**: Robots are also being designed to assist with the physical needs of elderly individuals. For example, robots can help patients with mobility issues stand up, move from one place to another, or get in and out of bed. This is particularly important as it reduces the risk of falls and injuries, which are a significant concern for the elderly.

o **Monitoring Health**: Robots and AI-powered systems are also used to monitor the health of elderly individuals, reminding them to take medications, tracking vital signs, and even alerting caregivers if something goes wrong. This can help reduce hospital readmissions and improve overall quality of life for elderly patients living at home.

3. **Robots in Diagnostics**

o **AI-powered Diagnostics**: In diagnostics, robots equipped with AI and machine learning algorithms are being used to analyze medical images, such as X-rays, MRIs, and CT scans. These robots help detect diseases such as cancer, heart conditions, and neurological disorders with greater accuracy and speed than human doctors alone.

o **How It Works**: AI systems are trained on large datasets of medical images, learning to identify subtle patterns that may indicate disease. These systems can often detect abnormalities at an

63

earlier stage than traditional methods, improving early detection rates and treatment outcomes.

o **Robotic Pathology**: Robots are also assisting in pathology, where they can analyze tissue samples to diagnose diseases like cancer. These robots can work around the clock, processing more samples and providing faster results to doctors.

Case Studies: Robotic Surgery, Robotic Exoskeletons

1. **Robotic Surgery: The da Vinci Surgical System**

   o **Overview**: One of the most prominent examples of robotic surgery is the **da Vinci Surgical System**. This robotic system allows surgeons to perform minimally invasive surgery with extreme precision. It has been used in various fields such as urology, gynecology, cardiothoracic surgery, and general surgery.

   o **How It Works**: The system consists of a robotic arm, a console for the surgeon to control, and a high-definition 3D camera. The surgeon sits at the console, where they control the robotic arms with their hands and foot pedals. The arms are equipped with tiny instruments and a camera that provide real-time, high-resolution images of the surgical area, offering greater visibility and precision than the human eye alone.

- o **Real-World Example**: In prostate cancer surgeries, the da Vinci system has been shown to reduce the risk of complications and allow for quicker recovery times. Surgeons can perform complex procedures like prostate removal with far less blood loss and a lower risk of infection than traditional open surgery.

2. **Robotic Exoskeletons: Empowering Paralyzed Patients**

   - o **Overview**: Robotic exoskeletons are wearable devices that use robotic technology to assist individuals with mobility impairments. These exoskeletons allow people with spinal cord injuries or conditions like paralysis to stand up and walk, significantly improving their quality of life.

   - o **How It Works**: Exoskeletons are made up of a frame that is worn on the body, with motors and sensors that help move the legs. The user controls the movement of the exoskeleton by shifting their weight or using a handheld controller. The technology relies on sensors that detect movement and sensors on the exoskeleton to adapt to the user's body and gait.

   - o **Real-World Example**: **ReWalk Robotics**, a company that produces robotic exoskeletons, has developed a system that allows paraplegic patients to walk. These exoskeletons use motorized joints at the hips and knees to simulate walking motions. In clinical trials, patients using ReWalk have shown improved cardiovascular health, muscle tone, and even psychological well-being due to their regained mobility.

3. **Exoskeletons in Rehabilitation: Ekso Bionics**

   o **Overview**: **Ekso Bionics** is another company that has developed a robotic exoskeleton that can be used for both rehabilitation and mobility assistance. This technology helps patients who have experienced strokes, spinal cord injuries, or other forms of paralysis to regain movement and rebuild muscle strength.

   o **How It Works**: The Ekso exoskeleton is designed to help patients who are unable to walk due to neurological impairments. It is controlled by the patient's movements or by a therapist to provide assistance in standing and walking. This can dramatically improve rehabilitation outcomes by helping patients to relearn motor skills and reduce the effects of muscle atrophy.

   o **Real-World Example**: In hospitals and rehabilitation centers, Ekso Bionics' devices have been used to help patients recover motor function after spinal cord injuries or strokes. Some patients have been able to regain the ability to stand and walk with assistance, and the devices are being used to encourage physical therapy and improve long-term outcomes.

Robots in healthcare are revolutionizing how we approach medicine, patient care, and rehabilitation. From robotic surgeries that minimize recovery times and improve precision to exoskeletons that help paralyzed individuals regain mobility, robotics are improving outcomes across the healthcare spectrum. Case studies such as the **da Vinci Surgical System** and **ReWalk Robotics** illustrate how these innovations are already changing lives, and as technology advances, robots will continue to play an even greater role in transforming healthcare for the better.

CHAPTER 9

AUTOMATION IN AGRICULTURE: SMART FARMING FOR A GROWING WORLD

How Automation is Revolutionizing Food Production

The agricultural industry has been gradually adopting automation technologies to keep pace with the growing global demand for food. With a rapidly increasing world population, the pressure to produce more food while using fewer resources is intensifying. Automation, driven by technologies like robotics, AI, IoT (Internet of Things), and data analytics, is playing a key role in revolutionizing how food is produced.

Automation in agriculture involves using machines, sensors, and software to streamline farming processes, increase efficiency, and reduce human labor. The goal is to make farming more sustainable, precise, and cost-effective, addressing challenges such as labor shortages, unpredictable weather, and the need to boost crop yields.

Some key ways in which automation is transforming agriculture include:

1. **Precision Farming**: Automation helps farmers manage their crops with greater precision, improving yield while reducing waste and the use of resources like water and fertilizers.

2. **Increased Efficiency**: Automated systems reduce the need for manual labor and minimize human errors, allowing for faster, more consistent farming operations.

3. **Sustainability**: By utilizing smart technology to optimize water usage, pesticide application, and soil health, automated farming systems contribute to more environmentally friendly farming practices.

Examples of Automated Tractors, Drones, and Crop Monitoring Systems

1. **Automated Tractors and Self-Driving Machinery**
   - **Overview**: One of the most significant advancements in farming automation is the development of **autonomous tractors** and self-driving machinery. These vehicles are designed to perform essential tasks like plowing, planting, and harvesting without human intervention.
   - **How It Works**: These autonomous tractors are equipped with GPS, sensors, and AI-powered

control systems to navigate fields. They can work around the clock, using precise data to perform tasks such as planting seeds at optimal depths and spacing. Autonomous tractors can also adjust their actions based on real-time data about soil conditions, weather, and crop types, improving efficiency and reducing the risk of human error.

- o **Real-World Example**: **John Deere** is one of the leading companies in autonomous farming machinery. Their autonomous tractor systems, like the **8R Tractor**, feature integrated GPS and advanced cameras that allow them to navigate fields, plow, and plant seeds autonomously. These tractors significantly reduce the need for human labor while improving the precision of fieldwork, such as seeding and fertilizing.

2. **Drones in Agriculture: Crop Monitoring and Spraying**

- o **Overview**: **Drones** have become a crucial tool in modern agriculture for monitoring crops, assessing soil health, and even spraying pesticides and fertilizers. Equipped with cameras, sensors, and GPS technology, drones provide a bird's-eye view of the farm, capturing valuable data to guide farming decisions.

o **How It Works**: Drones are deployed to fly over fields, capturing high-resolution images and videos that provide insight into crop health, growth patterns, and potential pest infestations. With the help of AI and data analytics, farmers can analyze this information to identify problem areas in the field, such as dry spots, nutrient deficiencies, or pest outbreaks.

o **Real-World Example**: **PrecisionHawk**, a leading drone manufacturer, offers a platform that combines drone technology with AI and machine learning to provide farmers with detailed insights into crop conditions. The platform can detect irregularities in plant growth, monitor irrigation levels, and even assist with crop mapping, helping farmers make data-driven decisions to maximize yield.

o Additionally, drones like those from **DJI** are also used for crop spraying. These drones can carry liquid fertilizers and pesticides, applying them precisely and efficiently, reducing the environmental impact of overuse and minimizing labor costs.

3. **Crop Monitoring Systems and Smart Sensors**

o **Overview**: In addition to drones and automated tractors, **crop monitoring systems** equipped with smart sensors are becoming increasingly common in agriculture. These systems allow farmers to track real-time data related to soil moisture, temperature, humidity, and even plant health, enabling them to make informed decisions and optimize farming practices.

- o **How It Works**: Smart sensors placed in the soil or attached to plants collect data on environmental factors such as temperature, humidity, soil composition, and nutrient levels. This data is then transmitted to a cloud platform, where AI systems analyze it to offer insights into when to water, irrigate, fertilize, or harvest crops.

- o **Real-World Example**: **CropX**, an ag-tech company, offers a soil sensor system that helps farmers monitor soil moisture and temperature in real time. This allows farmers to optimize irrigation schedules, improving water use efficiency and reducing waste. Similarly, **Arable** provides a weather station that collects data on various environmental factors, helping farmers assess the best times for planting and harvesting crops based on weather predictions.

4. **Robotic Harvesting**
- o **Overview**: Harvesting is one of the most labor-intensive tasks in agriculture, and robots are

beginning to step in to ease the burden. **Robotic harvesters** use advanced vision systems, AI, and machine learning to detect ripe fruits and vegetables and pick them with precision, allowing for faster, more efficient harvesting.

o **How It Works**: Robotic harvesters use sensors and cameras to identify ripe crops based on color, shape, and size. AI algorithms help the robot decide the best way to pick the fruit or vegetable without damaging it. For example, robotic arms and soft grippers are designed to gently pick produce like tomatoes, strawberries, and apples.

o **Real-World Example**: **FFRobotics** has developed a robotic system that can harvest apples. The robot uses AI to analyze the ripeness of the fruit and uses a gentle picking mechanism to remove the apples from trees without causing damage. This technology is particularly useful for crops that require delicate handling.

5. **Automated Irrigation Systems**

o **Overview**: Water management is a critical factor in farming, especially in regions where water is scarce or irregular. **Automated irrigation systems**, powered by IoT and AI, can optimize the watering of crops, ensuring that water is applied efficiently and only when needed.

o **How It Works**: Automated irrigation systems use sensors placed in the soil to monitor moisture levels. When the soil reaches a predefined dryness threshold, the system automatically activates the irrigation system to water the crops. These systems can also be programmed to adjust watering schedules based on weather forecasts or crop needs.

o **Real-World Example**: **Netafim**, a global leader in smart irrigation, offers drip irrigation systems that use sensors to monitor soil moisture and ensure precise water delivery. Their automated systems help farmers reduce water usage, which is crucial in arid regions where water conservation is essential.

Automation in agriculture is helping to transform food production, making it more efficient, sustainable, and precise. From **automated tractors** and **drones** that monitor crops and spray fertilizers, to **robotic harvesters** and **smart irrigation systems**, these innovations are optimizing farming practices and helping farmers feed a growing world. As automation technologies continue to advance, they hold the potential to improve food security, reduce resource

74

waste, and help build a more sustainable agricultural system for the future.

4o mini

• The Impact of Automation on Retail and E-commerce • How robots and AI are transforming retail experiences • Examples: Amazon's automated warehouses, cashier-less stores

Chapter 10: The Impact of Automation on Retail and E-commerce

How Robots and AI Are Transforming Retail Experiences

Automation, driven by robots and artificial intelligence (AI), is revolutionizing the retail and e-commerce industries by enhancing efficiency, reducing costs, and improving customer experiences. From the way products are stored and moved in warehouses to how customers shop online or in physical stores, automation is transforming every aspect of retail.

Automation in retail involves using robots, AI, and smart technologies to streamline tasks such as inventory management, order fulfillment, customer service, and in-store experiences. The goal is to make shopping faster, more personalized, and more efficient while reducing operational costs.

Key areas where automation is making an impact in retail include:

1. **Warehouse Automation**: Robots and AI systems are being used to automate inventory management, order fulfillment, and product sorting, allowing retailers to process orders quickly and accurately.
2. **Personalized Shopping**: AI analyzes customer data to offer tailored shopping experiences, recommendations, and targeted marketing, enhancing customer satisfaction and boosting sales.
3. **Checkout Automation**: Automation in the checkout process, such as self-checkout machines or cashier-less stores, reduces wait times and improves the efficiency of the shopping experience.

Examples: Amazon's Automated Warehouses, Cashier-less Stores

1. **Amazon's Automated Warehouses**
   o **Overview**: Amazon is at the forefront of using automation to enhance its e-commerce operations. The company's warehouses are a

prime example of how robots and AI are transforming logistics and order fulfillment.

- **How It Works**: Amazon employs **Kiva robots** (now known as **Amazon Robotics**) to help with inventory management and order picking. These robots use sensors and AI to navigate the warehouse, transporting shelves of products to human workers who then pick items for orders. The robots move quickly and efficiently, significantly reducing the time it takes to locate and retrieve products.

- **Robotic Sorting and Packaging**: Amazon's robots also help with sorting packages and placing them in the correct shipping areas. Once items are picked, they are moved to packing stations where robots assist in boxing and labeling packages for shipment.

- **AI for Demand Forecasting**: AI is also used in Amazon's warehouses to predict demand and optimize inventory. The system analyzes customer purchasing patterns, seasonality, and other factors to ensure that popular items are stocked in sufficient quantities, reducing stockouts and improving the efficiency of order fulfillment.

- o **Real-World Example**: In 2012, Amazon acquired **Kiva Systems**, which had developed robots designed to transport products around warehouses. Today, Amazon's fulfillment centers, including its massive facilities in places like Kentucky and California, use more than 100,000 robots to assist with everything from locating and retrieving inventory to sorting and packing orders. This automation has drastically reduced the time it takes for orders to be processed, allowing Amazon to offer fast shipping options like **Prime**.

2. **Cashier-less Stores**

   - o **Overview**: Cashier-less stores are becoming a growing trend in retail, especially with the rise of companies like **Amazon Go**. These stores use a combination of sensors, cameras, and AI to enable a checkout-free shopping experience, offering customers the ability to grab items and leave without having to wait in line or scan products.

   - o **How It Works**: In cashier-less stores, customers use a mobile app to enter the store and are tracked by cameras and sensors as they move around. The system uses AI and computer vision to detect the items that customers pick up, automatically adding them to a virtual shopping cart. When the customer is ready to leave, they simply walk out, and their account is charged for the items they've taken.

- o **Amazon Go**: One of the most famous examples of a cashier-less store is **Amazon Go**, which launched in 2016. Amazon Go uses a technology called **Just Walk Out** that combines AI, computer vision, and sensor fusion to track products as customers select them from the shelves. There are no traditional checkout lines, and customers are automatically charged via their Amazon account once they leave the store.

- o **Real-World Example**: Amazon Go stores have expanded to major cities like Seattle, Chicago, and New York, and they provide a seamless shopping experience, especially for busy consumers. This technology is slowly spreading to other retailers as well, such as **Walmart** and **7-Eleven**, who are exploring similar cashier-less concepts in their own stores.

3. **AI and Robotics in Customer Service**

- o **Overview**: AI and robotics are not only transforming back-end operations like order fulfillment and inventory management but also enhancing customer service in retail. AI-powered chatbots, virtual assistants, and robots are providing instant assistance to customers, improving response times, and reducing labor costs.

- o **How It Works: Chatbots** powered by AI are used on retail websites and mobile apps to interact with customers, answer questions, and guide them through the purchasing process. These chatbots can handle a wide range of tasks, from providing product recommendations to troubleshooting issues. Some chatbots even use **natural language processing (NLP)** to understand and respond to customer inquiries in a more human-like way.

- o **Robotic Store Assistants**: Retailers are also deploying robots in stores to assist customers with in-store navigation and product searches. For instance, **Pepper**, a humanoid robot, is used in some stores to greet customers, provide product information, and help customers find items. These robots are equipped with sensors and AI to understand customer queries and provide real-time assistance.

- o **Real-World Example**: In Japan, **SoftBank**'s **Pepper** robot is used in stores like **L'Oreal** and **Aldi** to greet customers, recommend products, and offer promotions. Meanwhile, in e-commerce, AI chatbots like **Sephora's Sephora Virtual Artist** use AI to suggest makeup products based on a customer's preferences or appearance, offering a more personalized shopping experience.

4. AI in Personalized Shopping and Recommendations

- o **Overview**: One of the biggest benefits of AI in retail is its ability to offer personalized shopping experiences. AI systems analyze customer data to provide tailored product recommendations, personalized marketing, and individualized shopping experiences both online and in-store.

- o **How It Works**: AI algorithms track customer behavior, purchase history, and browsing patterns to recommend products that a shopper is likely to be interested in. This personalized experience can extend to promotions, discounts, and even dynamic pricing based on customer preferences and demand.

- o **Real-World Example**: **Netflix** and **Amazon** are prime examples of companies that use AI to make personalized recommendations. On Amazon, the "Customers Who Bought This Also Bought" feature and **Amazon Prime Day** promotions are powered by AI, which analyzes large datasets to predict what customers will be interested in. In physical stores, AI-based systems can also suggest products based on customer preferences and past purchases.

Automation, powered by AI and robotics, is dramatically changing the landscape of retail and e-commerce. Companies like **Amazon** and **Walmart** are leading the way by leveraging technology to optimize everything from warehouse operations to in-store shopping experiences. With innovations such as **cashier-less stores, AI-powered customer service**, and **robotic fulfillment systems**, automation is streamlining operations, improving customer experiences, and making shopping faster, more personalized, and more efficient. As these technologies continue to evolve, they will play a critical role in shaping the future of retail, offering new levels of convenience and transforming the way we shop.

CHAPTER 11

AI AND DATA ANALYTICS: THE BACKBONE OF AUTOMATION

How Data Analytics Fuels Smarter Machines

Data analytics plays a crucial role in driving automation and making machines smarter. At the core of intelligent automation systems, data is used to inform decisions, predict outcomes, and continuously improve processes. **Artificial Intelligence (AI)** and **machine learning (ML)** rely on vast amounts of data to make sense of the world, learn from past experiences, and enhance the capabilities of machines.

Here's how data analytics fuels smarter machines:

1. **Data Collection**: Automated systems gather data through sensors, cameras, and other devices. This data can range from temperature readings to customer behavior patterns or sensor data from machines in a factory.

2. **Data Processing**: Once data is collected, it must be processed to make it usable. This is where AI and ML come in, using algorithms to filter, clean, and organize the data. Without proper processing, raw data is just information with no actionable insight.

83

3. **Pattern Recognition**: Through machine learning models, the system can identify patterns in the data. This allows machines to recognize trends, anomalies, and correlations that humans might miss. For example, predictive maintenance systems in factories analyze equipment data to foresee when a machine might break down.

4. **Predictive Analytics**: AI systems can use historical data to make predictions about future events. For example, in retail, predictive analytics can forecast product demand or customer buying behavior, allowing businesses to optimize inventory and supply chains.

5. **Real-time Decision Making**: Smarter machines rely on real-time data processing. In automated vehicles, for example, real-time data from sensors and cameras helps make split-second decisions on navigation, safety, and maneuvering.

Overall, data analytics allows machines to become more autonomous, making them capable of making data-driven decisions that improve efficiency, accuracy, and outcomes. Automation powered by data analytics can continuously optimize operations without human intervention, opening up new possibilities in various industries.

1. **Predictive Analytics in Manufacturing and Maintenance**
   - **Overview**: Predictive analytics is the use of data, statistical algorithms, and machine learning techniques to predict future outcomes based on historical data. In manufacturing, predictive analytics is widely used to anticipate equipment failures, reduce downtime, and optimize maintenance schedules.
   - **How It Works**: In a factory, machines are equipped with sensors that monitor things like temperature, vibration, and pressure. This data is collected and analyzed to predict when a machine is likely to fail or require maintenance. Rather than performing maintenance on a regular schedule or after a breakdown occurs, predictive analytics helps companies perform maintenance exactly when it's needed, based on real-time data and trends.
   - **Real-World Example: General Electric (GE)** uses predictive analytics in its industrial operations, particularly in its **Predix platform**, which collects data from turbines and jet engines.

By analyzing sensor data, GE can predict when components will need to be serviced, reducing downtime and saving costs. Similarly, **Siemens** uses predictive maintenance in its manufacturing plants to improve operational efficiency and minimize unexpected breakdowns.

2. **Customer Behavior Tracking in Retail**

   o **Overview**: In retail, customer behavior tracking is a key component of personalized shopping experiences. By analyzing data from customer interactions, purchases, browsing history, and more, businesses can understand consumer preferences, predict future behavior, and tailor marketing efforts.

   o **How It Works**: Retailers use AI-powered analytics to track how customers engage with their websites, mobile apps, and even physical stores. This data includes everything from how long a customer spends on a product page to which items are added to the shopping cart or purchased. Machine learning models then use this information to identify trends and provide personalized recommendations.

   o **Real-World Example**: **Amazon** is a prime example of a company that uses customer behavior tracking and predictive analytics to personalize shopping experiences. Amazon's recommendation engine analyzes past purchases, search history, and browsing patterns to suggest products a customer is likely to buy. Similarly, **Netflix** uses predictive analytics to recommend movies and TV shows based on a viewer's past watching behavior, keeping users engaged with content that matches their interests.

o **In Physical Stores**: Many brick-and-mortar stores are also adopting behavior tracking technologies. **Smart cameras** and **beacons** placed around stores can track foot traffic, customer movements, and even facial expressions to gauge customer interest and engagement with specific products. This data helps retailers adjust store layouts, optimize promotions, and provide real-time offers to customers.

3. **Predictive Analytics in E-commerce: Dynamic Pricing**

o **Overview**: Predictive analytics is increasingly being used in e-commerce to set dynamic prices based on real-time demand, competitor pricing, and consumer behavior. By analyzing data from a variety of sources, retailers can adjust prices instantly to maximize sales and revenue.

o **How It Works**: E-commerce platforms use AI-powered pricing engines that analyze factors like customer demand, market trends, inventory levels, and competitor pricing. If demand for a product is high and stock is limited, the price may increase. Alternatively, if there's an oversupply of a product or a competitor drops their price, the AI system may adjust the price downward.

o **Real-World Example**: **Airlines** and **hotel booking websites** have long used dynamic pricing models to adjust prices based on demand. Similarly, **Amazon** employs dynamic pricing for its products, frequently adjusting prices in response to real-time data about competitor prices, stock levels, and customer purchasing trends. This type of predictive pricing allows businesses to stay competitive and increase their revenue.

4. **AI in Financial Services: Fraud Detection and Risk Management**

o **Overview**: In the financial sector, AI and predictive analytics are being used for fraud detection, credit scoring, and risk management. By analyzing historical transaction data, AI systems can identify patterns of fraud, predict potential risks, and make real-time decisions to protect both businesses and customers.

- o **How It Works**: AI algorithms track transactions and look for anomalies or behavior that deviates from the norm, such as unusual spending patterns or large transfers. If a potential fraud event is detected, the system can trigger an alert or automatically block the transaction until further investigation is made.

- o **Real-World Example**: **MasterCard** uses predictive analytics to detect fraudulent activity on credit cards. Its AI system monitors transactions in real-time, analyzing patterns and flagging transactions that appear suspicious. Similarly, **American Express** uses AI to monitor cardholder behavior and predict potential risks, enhancing security for both customers and the company.

Data analytics is a fundamental backbone of automation, enabling machines to make smarter, data-driven decisions. Predictive analytics and customer behavior tracking are transforming industries like manufacturing, retail, and financial services by optimizing operations, improving customer experiences, and reducing costs. As AI continues to evolve, the role of data analytics will only become more integral to the development of smarter machines that enhance automation across industries.

CHAPTER 12

SMART FACTORIES: THE FUTURE OF MANUFACTURING

The Concept of Industry 4.0 and Smart Factories

Industry 4.0, often referred to as the **Fourth Industrial Revolution**, represents the transformation of manufacturing through automation, data exchange, and smart technologies. It marks the shift from traditional manufacturing methods to more efficient, flexible, and intelligent systems that leverage the power of **IoT (Internet of Things)**, **artificial intelligence (AI)**, **robotics**, **cloud computing**, and **big data analytics**.

The key concept behind **Industry 4.0** is the integration of cyber-physical systems (CPS) into manufacturing processes. These systems combine physical machines with digital technologies to create "smart" systems capable of independently controlling and monitoring production processes. The result is a more agile and efficient factory that can respond to changing demands in real-time, optimize resource usage, and maintain high levels of precision.

Smart factories, a core element of Industry 4.0, utilize **intelligent automation** to improve the production process. They rely on sensors, robots, and data-driven decision-making to optimize everything from production lines to supply chain management. These factories are interconnected, meaning that machines, systems, and even employees can communicate and collaborate seamlessly across the entire production environment.

Key components of Industry 4.0 in smart factories include:

1. **IoT-enabled Devices**: Machines, sensors, and equipment are interconnected and communicate data in real-time to optimize operations and maintenance.
2. **Cyber-Physical Systems**: These systems combine physical machines with computational elements to enable real-time monitoring, control, and decision-making.
3. **Artificial Intelligence (AI) and Machine Learning**: AI algorithms help predict outcomes, optimize workflows, and detect issues before they occur.
4. **Big Data Analytics**: The collection and analysis of vast amounts of data to identify trends, improve processes, and reduce downtime.
5. **Robotics and Automation**: The use of robots and automated systems to carry out repetitive, dangerous, or complex tasks with high precision and speed.

Industry 4.0 represents a paradigm shift that is transforming how factories operate, making them more efficient, flexible, and capable of meeting the demands of modern manufacturing.

Examples: Automated Assembly Lines, Predictive Maintenance

1. **Automated Assembly Lines**
   - **Overview**: Automated assembly lines are a cornerstone of modern smart factories. These lines utilize robots, conveyors, and automated machinery to perform repetitive tasks like assembling parts, welding, or packing products.
   - **How It Works**: In automated assembly lines, robots or automated machines are programmed to perform specific tasks with high precision. These systems can be configured to work 24/7, with minimal human intervention, reducing production time and increasing throughput. AI and sensors monitor the quality of each part being assembled, ensuring that defective items are identified and removed early in the process.
   - **Benefits**: Automated assembly lines improve efficiency, reduce human error, and increase production speed. These lines can also be easily

reconfigured to accommodate new products or production methods, offering greater flexibility.

o **Real-World Example**: **Tesla's Gigafactories** are a prime example of automated assembly lines. Tesla uses highly automated systems in their factories to produce electric vehicles, including robotic arms for tasks like welding, painting, and component assembly. These robots work with human operators to complete tasks at a much faster pace than traditional methods, increasing productivity and reducing costs.

2. **Robotic Process Automation (RPA) in Smart Factories**

o **Overview**: Robotic Process Automation (RPA) involves the use of robots to automate tasks that would otherwise be completed by human workers. In smart factories, RPA can be used for tasks like material handling, sorting, and packing.

o **How It Works**: RPA in manufacturing typically involves robots or automated machines that take over routine tasks. For example, robotic arms might be used to lift and place heavy components, reducing the physical strain on human workers. These systems are programmed to handle specific tasks and can work collaboratively with humans or other machines.

- o **Real-World Example: BMW's Spartanburg Plant** in South Carolina has implemented RPA to automate certain aspects of its manufacturing process, including the handling of parts during assembly. Robots are used to move parts along the production line, improving speed and efficiency while reducing the risk of injury to workers.

3. **Predictive Maintenance**
   - o **Overview**: Predictive maintenance is one of the most valuable applications of Industry 4.0 technology in smart factories. It uses sensors, data analytics, and AI to predict when machines or equipment are likely to fail, allowing for timely maintenance and reducing downtime.
   - o **How It Works**: Sensors are installed on factory equipment to monitor parameters such as temperature, vibration, pressure, and wear. This data is then analyzed in real-time by AI algorithms, which can detect anomalies and predict when a failure is likely to occur. Maintenance teams are alerted ahead of time, allowing them to address issues before they cause disruptions in the production process.
   - o **Benefits**: Predictive maintenance reduces the risk of unexpected equipment breakdowns, extends

the life of machines, and helps to avoid costly downtime. It also ensures that resources like spare parts and maintenance personnel are allocated efficiently, reducing operational costs.

- o **Real-World Example**: **Siemens** uses predictive maintenance in its smart factories to monitor the condition of production machines. The company's **MindSphere** platform collects data from sensors and analyzes it to predict when machines will need maintenance. This proactive approach has significantly reduced downtime and maintenance costs for Siemens.

4. **Smart Supply Chain Management**

- o **Overview**: Smart factories also use automation to streamline and optimize supply chains. Through IoT sensors, RFID tags, and data analytics, manufacturers can track the movement of materials and finished goods in real time, improving efficiency and reducing delays.

- o **How It Works**: In a smart supply chain, goods are tracked using RFID and sensors that provide real-time data on their location and condition. AI systems analyze this data to optimize inventory levels, predict demand, and ensure that raw materials arrive just in time for production.

- o **Real-World Example**: **Unilever** has adopted smart supply chain systems that use IoT and AI to track products from suppliers to manufacturing plants. By connecting different stages of the supply chain, Unilever is able to reduce lead times, optimize logistics, and improve inventory management. This helps them meet customer demand more efficiently while reducing costs and waste.

5. **3D Printing in Manufacturing**

- o **Overview**: 3D printing, also known as additive manufacturing, is an emerging technology in smart factories that allows for the creation of complex parts and components directly from digital models. This process eliminates the need for traditional manufacturing methods, which can be costly and time-consuming.

- o **How It Works**: 3D printers use computer-aided design (CAD) models to create objects layer by layer, using materials like plastic, metal, or composite materials. This allows for rapid prototyping, low-volume production, and even the creation of customized parts.

- o **Real-World Example**: **General Electric (GE)** uses 3D printing to create complex metal parts for jet engines. By using additive manufacturing, GE has been able to produce parts that are lighter, stronger, and more cost-effective than traditional manufacturing methods.

Smart factories, powered by Industry 4.0 technologies, are transforming the manufacturing landscape. Automated assembly lines, predictive maintenance, and smart supply chain management are optimizing production processes and creating more efficient, flexible, and sustainable factories. Companies like **Tesla**, **BMW**, and **Siemens** are leading the charge in adopting these advanced technologies, demonstrating how automation can revolutionize manufacturing operations. As these technologies continue to evolve, smart factories will become even more interconnected and intelligent, reshaping the future of manufacturing.

CHAPTER 13

ROBOTIC PROCESS AUTOMATION (RPA): STREAMLINING BUSINESS OPERATIONS

Defining RPA and Its Business Applications

Robotic Process Automation (RPA) refers to the use of software robots or "bots" to automate repetitive, rule-based tasks within business processes. RPA is designed to streamline operations by handling tasks that require human effort but are highly repetitive, manual, and time-consuming. These tasks might include data entry, invoice processing, report generation, and email handling.

Unlike traditional automation, RPA software does not require deep system integration or heavy changes to existing IT infrastructure. It interacts with applications through their user interface in the same way a human would, making it easy to implement without disrupting business workflows.

RPA is applied across various business functions, including:

1. **Data Entry and Data Processing**: RPA can automate data entry tasks by extracting information from emails, websites, or databases and inputting it into the appropriate systems.

2. **Customer Service**: RPA bots can respond to customer inquiries, process orders, and manage support tickets, allowing human agents to focus on more complex tasks.

3. **Invoice and Payment Processing**: Bots can be used to automatically generate invoices, process payments, and track accounts, reducing human error and speeding up financial workflows.

4. **Compliance and Reporting**: RPA can automate the generation of compliance reports, monitor regulations, and ensure adherence to standards without manual intervention.

RPA's benefits include increased productivity, accuracy, scalability, and cost savings. It reduces the burden on employees, allowing them to focus on higher-value tasks while automating routine processes that don't require human decision-making.

1. **RPA in Financial Services**

- o **Overview**: The financial services industry involves numerous repetitive tasks, such as processing transactions, managing accounts, and ensuring compliance with regulatory requirements. RPA has the potential to streamline many of these operations, reducing the need for human intervention and improving efficiency.

- o **How It Works**: RPA bots in the financial services industry can automate tasks like updating customer records, processing credit applications, handling claims, and managing internal audits. These bots can quickly perform tasks that would otherwise take hours, such as transferring data from one system to another or checking for errors in financial documents.

- o **Real-World Example**: **HSBC**, a major global bank, implemented RPA to automate its Know Your Customer (KYC) processes. RPA bots are used to verify customer identity and cross-check relevant data against global databases, reducing the time needed to onboard clients while ensuring compliance with financial regulations. This system has significantly improved the speed of customer onboarding and reduced the operational burden on employees.

- o **Additional Example**: **JP Morgan** also uses RPA for document processing. In its Contract Intelligence (COiN) platform, RPA bots help extract data from legal contracts, automating tasks that once took human employees days to complete. This automation has streamlined document review, allowing employees to focus on higher-level decision-making.

2. RPA in Human Resources (HR)

- o **Overview**: Human resources departments typically deal with a vast amount of administrative work, such as managing employee records, payroll processing, and recruitment. RPA has revolutionized HR operations by automating these time-consuming tasks, increasing accuracy and allowing HR teams to focus on employee engagement and strategy.

- o **How It Works**: In HR, RPA can automate tasks like processing new hire paperwork, managing payroll, handling benefits administration, and generating HR reports. It can also assist in recruitment by screening resumes, sending interview invitations, and updating candidate databases.

- o **Real-World Example**: **Cognizant**, a leading IT services company, implemented RPA to automate employee onboarding processes. The system now automatically processes new hires, sends welcome emails, sets up employee accounts, and completes payroll registration. As a result, the HR team has seen a significant reduction in manual work, improving both employee satisfaction and onboarding efficiency.

- o **Additional Example**: **Deloitte** has applied RPA to automate payroll processing for clients. The software bots handle data entry, calculations, and compliance checks, ensuring that employees are paid accurately and on time while reducing the workload for HR personnel. This has resulted in faster payroll cycles and fewer errors.

3. **RPA in Information Technology (IT)**

- o **Overview**: In IT operations, RPA is used to automate routine system maintenance, software deployment, and network monitoring. RPA helps reduce human error and ensures that critical IT processes are performed without delays.

- o **How It Works**: RPA bots in IT can automate tasks such as patch management, server monitoring, log file analysis, and backup processes. For example, RPA can be used to automatically apply security patches to software systems, ensuring that they are up-to-date without manual intervention.

- o **Real-World Example**: **Blue Prism**, a leader in RPA, has been used by **BP** (British Petroleum) to automate parts of its IT infrastructure management. The company uses RPA to monitor network performance and generate reports on system status. This has improved system uptime and made the company's IT operations more efficient, while reducing the need for IT staff to handle repetitive maintenance tasks.

- o **Additional Example**: **ServiceNow**, a cloud-based IT service management platform, uses RPA to automate various IT service processes. For example, the platform's RPA bots automate ticketing workflows, such as the handling of service requests and incident resolutions, ensuring quicker responses and more efficient resource allocation.

4. **RPA in IT Support: Automating User Account Management**

- o **Overview**: Managing user accounts and permissions across multiple systems is a critical but often tedious IT task. RPA is increasingly being used to automate account creation, modification, and deletion, as well as to enforce security protocols across platforms.

- o **How It Works**: RPA bots can automatically create user accounts, assign roles and permissions, and update access rights across multiple applications. This is especially useful in environments with high turnover or large-scale operations that require frequent updates to user information.

- o **Real-World Example**: **Accenture** implemented RPA in its IT department to automate the management of user accounts and access control across various applications. The bots help to streamline tasks like password resets, user authentication, and role assignments, which used to require significant time and manual effort from IT staff. As a result, the company has improved efficiency and security across its IT systems.

RPA is transforming business operations across various sectors, offering faster processing, reduced costs, and enhanced accuracy. In industries like **financial services**, **human resources**, and **information technology**, RPA is automating routine tasks, freeing up employees to focus on more strategic work. Companies like **HSBC, Cognizant,** and **BP** are leading the way by integrating RPA into their business processes, improving efficiency, and delivering better outcomes. As RPA technology evolves, its application will continue to grow, helping businesses operate more intelligently and cost-effectively.

CHAPTER 14

AUTOMATION IN LOGISTICS AND SUPPLY CHAIN MANAGEMENT

How Automation is Improving Efficiency in Logistics

Automation in logistics and supply chain management is revolutionizing the way goods are moved, stored, and delivered. From warehouses to transportation systems, automation is helping to streamline operations, reduce human error, and lower costs. As the demand for faster, more reliable delivery increases, automation offers solutions that enhance efficiency, speed, and flexibility.

Key benefits of automation in logistics include:

1. **Faster Order Fulfillment**: Automated systems in warehouses can pick, pack, and ship products much faster than human workers. This reduces the time it takes to process orders, leading to quicker delivery times.

2. **Improved Accuracy**: Automation eliminates manual errors, such as incorrect shipments or misplaced items. Robots and AI systems can track inventory with high

precision, ensuring that products are delivered exactly as ordered.

3. **Cost Reduction**: By automating repetitive tasks, businesses can reduce the need for human labor, cutting operational costs. Automation also optimizes resource utilization, such as storage space in warehouses, helping to minimize waste.

4. **Enhanced Flexibility**: Automation makes it easier to scale operations, especially when dealing with fluctuating demand. For instance, automated systems in warehouses can quickly adapt to higher volumes during peak seasons.

5. **Predictive Analytics**: Data-driven insights from automated systems help businesses make informed decisions about inventory management, route planning, and demand forecasting, further optimizing supply chain efficiency.

Examples: Automated Trucks, Drones for Last-Mile Delivery

1. **Automated Trucks: Revolutionizing Freight Transportation**

   o **Overview**: Autonomous trucks are one of the most exciting developments in logistics automation. These trucks can drive themselves with minimal or no human intervention, making long-haul freight transportation faster and more efficient.

108

- o **How It Works**: Automated trucks rely on a combination of sensors (like LIDAR, radar, and cameras), AI, and machine learning to navigate roads, avoid obstacles, and follow traffic laws. These trucks communicate with each other and central systems to optimize routes, ensure safety, and reduce fuel consumption.

- o **Benefits**: The use of autonomous trucks reduces the need for human drivers, minimizes the risk of human error (such as fatigue), and allows for more efficient long-distance travel. These trucks can operate around the clock, increasing the speed of freight delivery.

- o **Real-World Example**: **Waymo**, a subsidiary of Alphabet (Google's parent company), is one of the leaders in the autonomous truck space. Their self-driving trucks are already being tested in various states, and they have shown promise in improving safety and efficiency in freight transportation.

- o **Another Example**: **Tesla's Semi** truck, which is equipped with semi-autonomous driving capabilities, uses AI to assist drivers with navigation and safety features. Tesla plans to roll out fully autonomous versions of the truck in the near future, which will have the potential to

109

change the way freight logistics operate by significantly reducing the need for human labor and lowering transportation costs.

2. **Drones for Last-Mile Delivery**

o **Overview**: Drones are quickly becoming a popular solution for the "last-mile" delivery segment of logistics. The last mile is often the most expensive and time-consuming part of the delivery process, and drones are being used to solve this challenge by delivering packages directly to customers in urban or hard-to-reach areas.

o **How It Works**: Drones use GPS, sensors, and cameras to navigate through the air to deliver packages. They are typically designed to carry lightweight items and are programmed to follow specific delivery routes. Drones can avoid traffic, fly directly to the delivery destination, and drop off packages without the need for a human driver.

o **Benefits**: Drones significantly reduce delivery times, particularly for small packages. They also offer a more eco-friendly alternative to traditional delivery methods, as they don't rely on fuel-powered vehicles. Additionally, drones help reduce the cost of last-mile delivery, which can often make up a large portion of delivery expenses.

○ **Real-World Example**: **Amazon Prime Air** is one of the most well-known drone delivery programs in development. Amazon has been testing drones capable of delivering packages within 30 minutes of an order being placed. The drones use advanced navigation systems and sensors to ensure safe and accurate deliveries. Amazon plans to roll out drone deliveries in select regions in the coming years.

○ **Another Example**: **Wing**, a subsidiary of Alphabet, has launched drone delivery services in select areas, including parts of Australia and the U.S. The drones are capable of delivering food, medicine, and other small items directly to customers' doorsteps. Wing's system uses AI to manage the drones' flight paths and ensure safe, efficient deliveries.

3. **Automated Warehouses and Sorting Systems**

○ **Overview**: Warehouses are the backbone of supply chain operations, and automation in these facilities is transforming how goods are stored, sorted, and shipped. Automated warehouses use robots, conveyors, and AI to handle goods more efficiently than traditional systems.

- o **How It Works**: In an automated warehouse, robots are used to transport goods from one location to another, while conveyor belts and sorting systems organize products for packaging and shipping. AI-driven systems track inventory in real time, ensuring that products are stored in optimal locations and can be retrieved quickly. Automated machines are also used for tasks like picking and packing, reducing the need for human workers to handle products manually.

- o **Benefits**: Automated warehouses improve order accuracy, speed up processing times, and reduce labor costs. They also optimize space utilization, allowing warehouses to store more products in a smaller area.

- o **Real-World Example**: **Ocado**, a UK-based online grocery retailer, uses highly automated warehouses equipped with robots that handle everything from order picking to sorting and packing. The robots use AI to navigate the warehouse and ensure that the right products are picked at the right time. Ocado's automated systems have significantly reduced the time it takes to fulfill orders and improved overall customer satisfaction.

- o **Another Example**: **Alibaba's Cainiao Network** has developed an automated warehouse system in China that uses AI and robotics to process millions of packages daily. The system allows Cainiao to track packages in real time, improving efficiency and reducing shipping times.

4. **AI-Powered Supply Chain Optimization**

   - o **Overview**: AI is being used to optimize supply chain operations by analyzing data from multiple sources, predicting demand, and optimizing routes and inventories. AI algorithms can detect patterns, predict disruptions, and suggest optimal solutions in real-time.

   - o **How It Works**: AI analyzes data from various stages of the supply chain, including inventory levels, shipping schedules, and customer demand. Based on this analysis, AI systems can recommend actions such as adjusting inventory, rerouting deliveries, or scheduling maintenance to avoid disruptions.

   - o **Benefits**: AI-powered optimization leads to reduced lead times, lower costs, and better resource utilization. It helps businesses respond quickly to changes in demand, market conditions, and supply chain disruptions.

113

○ **Real-World Example: DHL** uses AI to optimize delivery routes, improving efficiency and reducing fuel costs. The AI system analyzes traffic patterns, weather conditions, and other variables to suggest the fastest routes for delivery trucks, helping DHL meet tight deadlines and improve service quality.

Automation in logistics and supply chain management is dramatically transforming the way goods are stored, moved, and delivered. From **autonomous trucks** that improve long-haul freight efficiency to **drones** that speed up last-mile delivery, automation is making logistics faster, more cost-effective, and environmentally friendly. Companies like **Amazon**, **Wing**, and **Ocado** are leading the way, demonstrating how automation can optimize operations and create more efficient supply chains. As technology continues to advance, automation will play an even greater role in shaping the future of logistics.

CHAPTER 15

THE ETHICS OF AUTOMATION: WHAT HAPPENS TO JOBS?

Exploring the Ethical Implications of Automation in the Workforce

The rapid advancement of automation, particularly with the rise of AI, robotics, and other technologies, has sparked concerns about its impact on employment and the workforce. While automation offers significant benefits, such as increased efficiency, productivity, and cost savings, it also raises ethical questions about job displacement, economic inequality, and the social responsibility of businesses and governments.

One of the most pressing ethical concerns is the **potential for job loss**. Many routine and manual jobs, such as those in manufacturing, retail, and customer service, are increasingly being replaced by machines. The fear is that as automation expands, large segments of the population, especially low-skill workers, could face unemployment without clear opportunities for retraining or new employment.

Here are some of the ethical implications of automation on the workforce:

1. **Job Displacement**: Automation can eliminate jobs, especially in industries with repetitive tasks. Workers in roles like assembly line positions, clerical work, and retail may face challenges in adapting to a world where robots and AI systems perform many of these tasks.

2. **Economic Inequality**: Automation could widen the gap between the skilled and unskilled workforce. Highly skilled workers in tech, engineering, and data science may thrive in an automated world, but those without specialized skills may struggle to find employment.

3. **Human Dignity and Purpose**: Many people derive a sense of purpose and dignity from their work. If automation reduces the number of jobs available or devalues certain types of work, it can lead to issues related to mental health and a loss of personal fulfillment.

4. **Impact on Developing Economies**: For countries where manufacturing and manual labor are dominant industries, automation could have a disproportionate impact, potentially leading to economic instability and widening the wealth gap between developed and developing nations.

Despite these concerns, it's important to note that automation is not inherently harmful to jobs. The ethical challenge is not about whether automation is good or bad, but rather how we manage and transition to a more automated workforce.

How Automation Can Create New Job Roles and Industries

While automation has the potential to replace certain jobs, it also presents opportunities for creating new roles and industries. As technology evolves, so do the skillsets required, leading to new jobs that didn't exist before.

1. **Creation of New Job Categories**
   o **Tech-Specific Roles**: As automation becomes more integrated into industries, the demand for skilled workers in fields like AI development, robotics engineering, and data science will continue to grow. New job categories, such as **AI ethicists**, **robot operators**, and **machine learning engineers**, are already emerging.
   o **Human-Machine Collaboration**: While robots and AI systems take over repetitive tasks, many workers will be needed to supervise, maintain, and collaborate with these systems. For example, **robotics technicians** and **automation supervisors** will play key roles in ensuring machines are running smoothly and making adjustments when necessary.

- o **Customer Experience and Services**: With automation handling many of the operational tasks, businesses will need more employees focused on customer relationships, emotional intelligence, and personalized service. Jobs like **customer experience designers, relationship managers**, and **service consultants** will thrive in industries where human interaction adds value.

2. **Shift to Higher-Value Jobs**

- o Automation encourages the shift from low-skill, repetitive jobs to higher-skill roles that require critical thinking, creativity, and problem-solving. In industries like healthcare, education, and entertainment, automation can provide workers with more time to focus on tasks that require human ingenuity.

- o **Healthcare**: In the healthcare industry, robots and AI can assist with diagnosis, surgery, and patient monitoring. As automation takes over routine medical tasks, healthcare workers, such as **nurses, physicians**, and **care coordinators**, can devote more time to patient care, research, and complex decision-making.

- o **Education**: Teachers and instructors may see their roles evolve as AI and automation help with administrative tasks like grading, scheduling, and

118

tutoring. Educators will be able to spend more time focusing on creative lesson plans and fostering students' critical thinking skills.

o **Entertainment and Creativity**: While AI can generate content like music, art, and literature, it still lacks the emotional and cultural context that human creativity brings. Automation will allow **artists**, **writers**, and **designers** to focus more on ideation and innovation, leaving repetitive tasks to machines.

3. **New Industries and Business Models**

o As automation creates new opportunities in different sectors, entirely new industries and business models are emerging. For example, **autonomous vehicle technology** is creating demand for roles in transportation and logistics, including **self-driving vehicle technicians**, **vehicle safety analysts**, and **logistics managers** who will work with AI-driven fleets.

o **AI and Big Data**: Industries focused on AI and data analytics are also expanding. Companies specializing in **AI training**, **machine learning model development**, and **data engineering** are creating thousands of new job opportunities that require specialized skills.

- o **Sustainable Technologies**: Automation is playing a crucial role in advancing sustainable practices, such as renewable energy and environmental monitoring. New job opportunities are arising in sectors like **clean energy** and **environmental engineering**, where automation systems can optimize energy consumption, waste management, and resource use.

4. **The Role of Education and Reskilling**

- o To adapt to the changing workforce, education and reskilling programs will be critical. As automation shifts the types of work available, there will be a growing need for training in digital literacy, coding, data analysis, and machine learning. Workers who can adapt to these new roles will be in high demand.

- o Governments and businesses are beginning to recognize the need for **retraining initiatives**. Programs designed to help workers transition to new industries or roles are already being implemented. For example, **Amazon** has invested in **Amazon Upskilling** programs to retrain employees in areas such as cloud computing, data science, and IT support, preparing them for the future job market.

Conclusion

While the ethical concerns surrounding automation, particularly in terms of job displacement, are valid, the integration of automation into the workforce is not a zero-sum game. Automation, when managed responsibly, has the potential to create new industries, job roles, and opportunities for growth. The challenge lies in ensuring that workers have the skills, support, and resources they need to transition into these new roles.

By focusing on reskilling, creating new job categories, and fostering industries that complement automated systems, we can ensure that automation becomes a force for positive change in the workforce. As society navigates the impact of automation, ethical considerations such as job displacement, economic inequality, and human dignity should be addressed through thoughtful policies, training programs, and strategic workforce planning. Ultimately, automation can lead to a more dynamic, efficient, and inclusive economy if we are proactive in managing its integration into the workplace.

CHAPTER 16

CHALLENGES AND LIMITATIONS OF AUTOMATION

Key Obstacles: Cost, Regulation, and Technological Barriers

While automation offers significant benefits such as increased efficiency, reduced costs, and improved precision, it also comes with its own set of challenges and limitations. These obstacles must be addressed for automation to be successfully implemented across various industries. Key barriers include **cost**, **regulation**, and **technological limitations**.

1. **Cost**

   o **Initial Investment**: One of the primary challenges of automation is the high initial cost of implementing automated systems. From purchasing robotic equipment to integrating AI software and sensors, the upfront investment can be significant. For small and medium-sized businesses, the cost of automation may be prohibitive, even though it can lead to long-term savings and efficiencies.

- ○ **Maintenance and Upkeep**: In addition to the initial setup, maintaining and servicing automated systems can be expensive. Robots and AI systems require regular updates, repairs, and calibrations to stay operational. Over time, these costs can add up, especially if the technology becomes outdated or needs to be replaced.

- ○ **Real-World Example**: **Ford Motor Company** faced significant challenges when implementing automation in its manufacturing plants. In the 1960s, Ford introduced automated machinery to speed up production lines. However, the costs of maintaining and updating these systems outweighed the benefits, leading to a reevaluation of their automation strategy. Today, while automation is an integral part of their operations, Ford continues to balance the cost-benefit analysis in their production facilities.

2. **Regulation**

- ○ **Legal and Safety Concerns**: Automation often raises regulatory and legal challenges, particularly in areas like autonomous vehicles, drones, and healthcare robots. Governments need to create and update laws and regulations to address safety standards, liability, and ethical concerns related to the use of automation. In some cases, regulations can be slow to catch up with technological advancements, which can hinder the adoption of automation.

- o **Worker Protections and Employment Laws**: The displacement of workers due to automation can lead to calls for stronger worker protection laws. Governments and industries may need to enact policies to ensure that displaced workers have access to retraining programs and unemployment benefits. Additionally, labor unions may push for protections for workers who are at risk of being replaced by robots.

- o **Real-World Example**: The rollout of **autonomous trucks** has faced significant regulatory challenges in various countries. While companies like **Waymo** and **Tesla** have made significant progress in developing self-driving technology, regulatory bodies have been slow to approve their widespread use. In the U.S., the Department of Transportation and state-level authorities are still debating how to establish safety standards and liability regulations for self-driving vehicles, causing delays in adoption.

3. **Technological Barriers**

- o **Limitations of Current Technology**: Although automation technology has made significant strides, there are still many limitations, especially in complex or unpredictable environments. For example, robots and AI systems struggle with tasks that require human-like judgment, emotional intelligence, and creativity. In industries like healthcare and customer service, human intervention is still essential for tasks that involve complex decision-making, empathy, or adaptability to changing situations.

o **Integration with Legacy Systems**: Many businesses rely on legacy systems that were not designed with automation in mind. Integrating new automated systems with older infrastructure can be challenging and costly. It may require significant re-engineering of existing processes and systems, which can be time-consuming and disruptive.

o **Real-World Example**: **Amazon's attempt at cashier-less stores**, using Amazon Go technology, faced significant challenges when it first launched. While the technology was impressive, it struggled with detecting certain items being purchased, particularly when customers placed multiple items into bags or moved them between shelves. The system's sensors and AI algorithms had difficulty

125

distinguishing between the different products, leading to frustrations for customers and delays in the rollout of the technology.

Real-World Examples of Automation Failures and Setbacks

1. **Autonomous Vehicles: Uber's Self-Driving Car Incident**

   o **Overview**: One of the most high-profile automation failures occurred in 2018 when an autonomous Uber vehicle struck and killed a pedestrian in Tempe, Arizona. This incident raised significant concerns about the safety and reliability of self-driving technology.

   o **Cause**: The vehicle's sensors failed to detect the pedestrian in time, and the human safety driver in the vehicle was unable to intervene quickly enough. The incident revealed weaknesses in both the sensor technology and the AI system's ability to recognize pedestrians in certain conditions, highlighting the challenges of automating decision-making in complex, real-world scenarios.

   o **Impact**: The incident led to a temporary halt in Uber's autonomous vehicle testing and increased scrutiny of the technology's safety. It also spurred further debate on the ethics of deploying autonomous vehicles and the responsibility of developers and manufacturers in ensuring safety before releasing such technology to the public.

2. **Amazon's Automated Warehouses: Robotic Arm Failures**

- o **Overview**: While **Amazon Robotics** has transformed the e-commerce giant's warehouses, not all automation efforts have been smooth. In the early days of adopting robotic systems in its fulfillment centers, Amazon faced several challenges.

- o **Cause**: One example of a failure occurred when robotic arms malfunctioned, resulting in damaged products and delays in order fulfillment. The robots used in Amazon's warehouses were designed to move products from shelves to packing stations, but software glitches and mechanical failures sometimes caused the robots to mishandle items or run into obstacles, leading to operational inefficiencies.

- o **Impact**: Amazon has since worked to improve the reliability of its robots and AI systems. However, this early setback demonstrated that automation technology still requires fine-tuning and that unexpected failures can disrupt even the most advanced systems. It also highlighted the need for backup systems and human oversight in highly automated environments.

3. **Artificial Intelligence: IBM Watson's Healthcare Setback**

   o **Overview**: **IBM Watson for Oncology** aimed to revolutionize healthcare by assisting doctors in diagnosing and treating cancer. The AI system was designed to analyze medical records, research papers, and clinical data to recommend personalized treatment plans for patients.

   o **Cause**: Despite the initial promise, the AI system struggled with real-world implementation. It was found to provide incorrect treatment recommendations due to insufficient data quality, inaccurate training, and the complexity of interpreting medical data. In several cases, Watson's recommendations did not align with best practices, and some patients received incorrect or harmful treatments.

   o **Impact**: IBM faced significant setbacks in rolling out Watson for Oncology, and many hospitals discontinued using the system. The failure highlighted the challenges of applying AI in healthcare, where errors can have serious consequences, and underscored the importance of

128

data quality and the need for human oversight in critical industries.

While automation offers immense potential, its challenges and limitations must not be overlooked. High initial costs, regulatory hurdles, and technological barriers can slow down or derail automation projects, as seen in the cases of **Uber's self-driving car incident**, **Amazon's warehouse failures**, and **IBM Watson's healthcare setbacks**. These real-world examples emphasize the need for continued development, testing, and oversight in automation technologies. As industries continue to invest in automation, addressing these challenges head-on will be crucial to ensuring the success and safety of future automation initiatives.

CHAPTER 17

HOW SMART MACHINES LEARN: THE BASICS OF MACHINE LEARNING AND DEEP LEARNING

Introduction to Machine Learning and Neural Networks

Machine learning (ML) and deep learning (DL) are key technologies that enable **smart machines** to learn from data and make decisions without explicit programming. These techniques, part of the broader field of **artificial intelligence (AI)**, allow systems to improve their performance over time as they process more information, making them essential in the development of autonomous systems and smart applications.

Machine Learning (ML) refers to the ability of machines to learn from data, identify patterns, and make predictions or decisions based on that data. ML algorithms are designed to automatically detect insights and improve performance as more data becomes available.

Deep Learning (DL) is a subset of machine learning that uses **neural networks**, inspired by the human brain's structure, to model complex patterns and decision-making processes. Deep learning excels at processing large volumes of unstructured data, such as images, video, and natural language, and is a driving force behind advanced AI applications.

Key Concepts in Machine Learning

1. **Supervised Learning**: This is the most common type of machine learning, where the algorithm is trained on a labeled dataset. Each piece of input data has a corresponding correct output. The model learns to map inputs to outputs during training and then generalizes to predict new, unseen data.

   o **Example**: A supervised learning algorithm might be trained on thousands of photos of cats and dogs, labeled as "cat" or "dog." After training, the model can predict whether a new photo shows a cat or a dog.

2. **Unsupervised Learning**: In this approach, the machine is given data without explicit labels. The algorithm tries to identify patterns and structures within the data, such as grouping similar items or reducing dimensions to find simpler representations of the data.

o **Example**: An unsupervised learning model could analyze customer data to segment users into different groups based on purchasing behavior, without being told what those groups are in advance.

3. **Reinforcement Learning**: In reinforcement learning, an agent learns to make decisions by interacting with its environment and receiving feedback in the form of rewards or penalties. The agent aims to maximize cumulative reward over time by choosing actions that lead to positive outcomes.

   o **Example**: Reinforcement learning is often used in training AI to play games like chess or Go, where the system learns strategies through trial and error, gradually improving its performance.

Neural Networks and Deep Learning

Neural networks are the backbone of deep learning, and they consist of layers of **artificial neurons** that process information. Each layer of neurons transforms the input data through a series of weighted connections and activation functions, gradually learning higher-level features.

1. **Artificial Neural Networks (ANNs)**: A simple neural network consists of three types of layers:

- o **Input layer**: Receives the raw input data.
- o **Hidden layers**: Intermediate layers that process the data and extract features.
- o **Output layer**: Produces the model's prediction or decision.

2. **Deep Learning Networks**: Deep learning involves training neural networks with many layers (deep neural networks). These networks can recognize complex patterns in data, such as identifying objects in images or understanding human speech in natural language processing tasks.

- o **Convolutional Neural Networks (CNNs)**: These networks are particularly effective for image and video processing. They can automatically detect features like edges, textures, and shapes, making them widely used in computer vision applications like facial recognition.
- o **Recurrent Neural Networks (RNNs)**: RNNs are used for sequence prediction tasks, such as language modeling, time series forecasting, and speech recognition, due to their ability to maintain a memory of previous inputs in the sequence.

Real-Life Applications: AI in Recommendation Systems, Facial Recognition

1. **AI in Recommendation Systems**

   o **Overview**: Recommendation systems are one of the most common applications of machine learning and deep learning. These systems analyze user behavior and preferences to recommend products, content, or services that a user is likely to enjoy or find useful.

   o **How It Works**:

     ▪ In **collaborative filtering**, recommendation systems analyze user behavior, such as purchase history or viewing preferences, and suggest items based on what similar users liked.

     ▪ In **content-based filtering**, the system recommends items similar to what the user has previously interacted with, based on item attributes like genre, author, or style.

     ▪ **Hybrid models** combine both methods to improve recommendations by leveraging both user data and item features.

   o **Real-World Example**:

134

- **Netflix** uses machine learning algorithms to recommend movies and TV shows to users based on their viewing history. The system analyzes patterns in the data, such as the genres and actors that users prefer, and suggests content accordingly.

- **Amazon** also uses recommendation algorithms to suggest products based on past purchases, browsing history, and user reviews. This personalized approach helps Amazon increase sales by offering products that are more likely to appeal to individual customers.

2. **Facial Recognition**

   o **Overview**: Facial recognition technology uses machine learning and deep learning to identify and verify individuals based on their facial features. This technology has become widely used in security systems, social media, and customer service.

   o **How It Works**: Facial recognition systems use **Convolutional Neural Networks (CNNs)** to analyze images or videos of faces. The system extracts key facial features, such as the distance between the eyes, nose shape, and jawline, and creates a unique facial signature. This signature is

135

then compared to a database of known faces to make an identification or verification decision.

○ **Real-World Example**:

- **Apple's Face ID** system uses facial recognition to unlock iPhones. It maps the user's face using infrared sensors and compares it to a stored 3D model of the user's face to ensure a match.

- **Facebook** employs facial recognition to tag individuals in photos. It uses deep learning algorithms to detect faces in images, even if the person has not been tagged before. The system can match newly uploaded photos with existing ones in its database to suggest tags automatically.

- **China's Facial Recognition in Public Surveillance**: In China, facial recognition technology is used for surveillance and law enforcement. The technology helps authorities monitor public spaces, identify suspects, and improve security measures. While effective, this widespread use of facial recognition has sparked concerns about privacy and surveillance.

3. **AI in Healthcare: Diagnostic Tools**

- o **Overview**: In healthcare, AI and deep learning are revolutionizing diagnostics by analyzing medical images, identifying patterns, and predicting disease outcomes with high accuracy. Deep learning models, particularly CNNs, are used to detect abnormalities such as tumors, fractures, or retinal issues in medical images.

- o **How It Works**: AI models are trained on large datasets of medical images, including X-rays, MRIs, and CT scans. The system learns to detect various conditions by recognizing patterns that indicate potential health issues.

- o **Real-World Example**:
  - **Google Health** developed an AI system that uses deep learning to detect breast cancer in mammograms. The system has shown to be as accurate as radiologists in detecting cancer, potentially speeding up diagnosis and improving early detection.
  - **Zebra Medical Vision** is using AI to read medical images and help radiologists diagnose diseases. Its AI models have been successful in detecting conditions like osteoporosis, cardiovascular disease, and certain

137

cancers, assisting doctors in making faster and more accurate diagnoses.

Machine learning and deep learning are at the heart of many modern AI applications, enabling machines to process data, learn from it, and make decisions with minimal human intervention. **Recommendation systems** and **facial recognition** are just two examples of how these technologies are transforming industries, from e-commerce to security and healthcare. As AI continues to advance, its potential to change the way we interact with technology and make decisions will only expand, paving the way for more intelligent and autonomous systems.

CHAPTER 18

THE ROLE OF HUMAN-ROBOT COLLABORATION

How Humans and Robots Can Work Together

Human-robot collaboration, or **cobots** (collaborative robots), represents a shift in how robots are integrated into the workplace. Unlike traditional industrial robots that work in isolation or behind barriers for safety, cobots are designed to work alongside human operators. These robots are equipped with advanced sensors, AI, and safety features that allow them to interact directly with people, enhancing productivity and efficiency while maintaining a safe working environment.

Cobots can assist with tasks that are either too dangerous, repetitive, or physically demanding for humans, while still leveraging human capabilities like judgment, creativity, and decision-making. The combination of human intelligence and the physical strength or precision of robots creates a powerful partnership that can improve both the quality of work and workplace dynamics.

Key aspects of human-robot collaboration include:

1. **Safety**: Cobots are designed with safety in mind, utilizing sensors, vision systems, and force-limiting features to ensure that they do not harm human workers, even in close proximity.

2. **Flexibility**: Cobots are often flexible and easy to reprogram, allowing them to take on different tasks as needed. This adaptability makes them suitable for environments where tasks may change frequently.

3. **Enhanced Productivity**: Robots can handle repetitive or labor-intensive tasks, while humans can focus on more complex, higher-level tasks. This division of labor enhances efficiency and reduces human fatigue, improving overall productivity.

4. **Skills Augmentation**: Cobots can assist workers by performing physically demanding tasks, such as lifting heavy objects, which allows humans to focus on tasks that require cognitive skills, such as problem-solving and decision-making.

Examples: Collaborative Robots (Cobots) in Manufacturing

1. **Universal Robots (UR)**
   o **Overview**: **Universal Robots**, one of the leading manufacturers of cobots, offers a range of robots designed to work safely alongside human

operators in industrial settings. These cobots are lightweight, flexible, and easy to program, making them ideal for small and medium-sized enterprises (SMEs) looking to automate their operations.

- o **How It Works**: Universal Robots' cobots can be programmed to perform a variety of tasks, such as assembly, welding, packaging, and quality control. The robots are equipped with advanced safety features, including force sensors that stop the robot's movement if it detects an obstruction or collision with a human.

- o **Real-World Example**: In **automobile manufacturing**, a company might use a cobot from Universal Robots to assist with repetitive tasks such as assembling car parts or installing screws. The cobot can work side-by-side with humans, performing the physically demanding tasks, while humans handle more intricate work like quality checks and adjustments.

2. **ABB's YuMi**

- o **Overview**: **YuMi** by ABB is another example of a cobot designed for human-robot collaboration. It is known for its flexibility, precision, and safety features, and is used in various industries, including electronics assembly and consumer goods manufacturing.

○ **How It Works**: YuMi is equipped with a two-arm design that allows it to work seamlessly with human operators. Its lightweight design and soft-grip arms enable it to perform tasks such as assembly, material handling, and quality inspection in close proximity to people. The robot can stop immediately if it senses any contact with a human, ensuring safety during interactions.

○ **Real-World Example**: In **electronics assembly**, YuMi is used to assemble small parts like circuit boards. The cobot performs delicate tasks such as placing components onto the board with high precision, while a human worker performs other tasks like inspecting the assembly for defects. The collaboration results in faster production and reduced human error.

3. **Rethink Robotics' Baxter and Sawyer**

○ **Overview**: **Baxter** and **Sawyer**, developed by **Rethink Robotics**, are designed specifically for human-robot collaboration in manufacturing and production environments. Both robots are equipped with advanced sensors, cameras, and AI capabilities that allow them to work safely and interactively with human colleagues.

- **How It Works**: Baxter is a larger, two-armed robot designed for tasks such as material handling and packaging, while Sawyer is a more agile, single-armed robot ideal for tasks requiring precision, like assembly or machine tending. Both robots can learn from human guidance and can be easily reprogrammed for different tasks, making them adaptable for a wide range of applications.

- **Real-World Example**: In **food production**, Sawyer might assist workers with tasks such as sorting and packaging food products, working alongside humans who handle tasks like inspection and logistics. Its high precision allows it to perform tasks that require careful handling, reducing human error and increasing efficiency.

4. **KUKA LBR iiwa**

- **Overview**: **KUKA**'s **LBR iiwa** (Leichtbauroboter IIWA) is a sensitive, lightweight robot designed specifically for close human interaction. The LBR iiwa uses force sensors in each joint to allow for safe, precise interactions with humans and delicate tasks.

- **How It Works**: The LBR iiwa can work collaboratively with human workers on tasks that require high precision and sensitivity, such as

143

assembly, packaging, or medical device manufacturing. The robot can adjust its movements based on the force feedback it receives, making it ideal for delicate applications.

o **Real-World Example**: In the **medical device industry**, the LBR iiwa can assist with assembling small components, such as those found in surgical tools, where precision is critical. The robot can work alongside human operators, taking on the repetitive or physically demanding tasks, while the human workers focus on quality control and other higher-level functions.

5. **Collaborative Robots in Warehouse Automation**

o **Overview**: In warehouse settings, cobots are increasingly being used to assist with tasks like order picking, sorting, and packing. These robots can work alongside human employees to increase throughput, reduce errors, and improve overall efficiency in logistics operations.

o **How It Works**: Cobots in warehouses use AI, vision systems, and sensors to navigate shelves, pick products, and pack them for shipment. They can communicate with human workers to coordinate tasks and ensure that orders are fulfilled quickly and accurately. In some cases, cobots can even be reprogrammed to adapt to different types of inventory, providing flexibility in dynamic environments.

o **Real-World Example**: **GreyOrange**, a robotics company, provides collaborative robots for warehouses that can assist with picking and sorting. These robots work in close proximity to human workers, taking on physically demanding tasks, while the humans perform activities such as quality inspection, problem-solving, and packaging.

Human-robot collaboration is transforming industries by combining the best of human abilities—creativity, decision-making, and adaptability—with the precision, strength, and efficiency of robots. Cobots, such as **Universal Robots**, **ABB's YuMi**, and **KUKA's LBR iiwa**, are just a few examples of how robots are designed to work alongside humans to improve productivity, safety, and overall efficiency. As automation continues to evolve, the future of work will likely involve more human-robot collaboration, where machines take over repetitive tasks, and humans focus on higher-level problem-solving and decision-making.

145

CHAPTER 19

SMART CITIES: AUTOMATION FOR URBAN DEVELOPMENT

How Automation is Transforming Urban Living

Smart cities are urban areas that use automation and technology to enhance the quality of life for their residents, improve sustainability, and streamline city operations. By integrating **IoT (Internet of Things)**, **artificial intelligence (AI)**, **big data**, and **automation**, smart cities are becoming more efficient, responsive, and livable.

Automation plays a central role in the development of smart cities by optimizing infrastructure, services, and resources. From traffic management to waste disposal, automation technologies allow cities to respond to real-time data and adapt their operations accordingly, leading to a reduction in costs, energy usage, and pollution. These advancements not only make cities more efficient but also create a safer, healthier, and more sustainable environment for residents.

Key benefits of automation in smart cities include:

1. **Efficiency**: Automation optimizes city operations, reducing energy consumption, improving resource allocation, and cutting down operational costs.
2. **Sustainability**: By managing resources like water and energy more effectively, smart cities can reduce their environmental impact and promote greener living.
3. **Safety and Security**: Automated systems in surveillance, law enforcement, and emergency response help cities become safer by enabling quicker responses to incidents.
4. **Quality of Life**: Smart city technologies, such as automated traffic management and smart utilities, enhance the convenience and comfort of urban living, offering residents more control over their daily lives.

Examples: Traffic Management, Smart Utilities, Waste Management

1. **Automated Traffic Management**
   o **Overview**: **Traffic management** is one of the most critical challenges in urban areas, particularly as cities continue to grow in size and population. Automation and AI are being used to optimize traffic flow, reduce congestion, and improve road safety.
   o **How It Works**: Smart traffic management systems use real-time data from sensors, cameras, GPS, and vehicle tracking systems to monitor

traffic patterns and adjust signals dynamically. AI algorithms analyze traffic flow, predict congestion, and automatically adjust traffic light timings to improve the movement of vehicles and pedestrians.

- o **Benefits**: Automated traffic systems reduce congestion, lower fuel consumption, and improve air quality by minimizing idling times. These systems can also provide real-time information to drivers about traffic conditions, accidents, and alternative routes, enhancing travel efficiency.

- o **Real-World Example**: **Singapore** is one of the leading cities in adopting automated traffic management. The city uses an extensive network of sensors, cameras, and data analytics to manage traffic flow. Singapore's **ERP (Electronic Road Pricing)** system uses real-time data to adjust toll prices based on traffic conditions, encouraging drivers to take alternative routes during peak times and reducing congestion in busy areas.

2. **Smart Utilities**

- o **Overview**: **Smart utilities** leverage automation, sensors, and AI to monitor and manage essential urban services like water, electricity, and gas. These systems help optimize resource distribution, ensure efficient usage, and reduce wastage.

- o **How It Works**: Smart meters and sensors are installed throughout the city's infrastructure to collect real-time data on water and energy consumption. This data is analyzed by AI systems to detect inefficiencies, predict demand, and provide insights into how to optimize energy use across the city. For example, smart grids help balance electricity supply and demand, while automated irrigation systems manage water usage more effectively.

- o **Benefits**: Automation in utilities reduces waste, ensures efficient resource distribution, and provides citizens with better control over their usage. These systems can also detect leaks, power outages, and inefficiencies, allowing for quicker responses to potential problems.

- o **Real-World Example**: **Barcelona**, Spain, has implemented a **smart water management system** that uses sensors to monitor water consumption in real-time. The city uses this data to optimize water distribution, detect leaks, and reduce waste. In addition, **smart lighting** systems in Barcelona adjust streetlights' brightness based on the time of day, weather, and pedestrian activity, leading to energy savings and improved sustainability.

3. **Smart Waste Management**

   o **Overview**: Waste management is another critical area where automation is transforming urban living. Smart waste management systems use sensors, robotics, and AI to optimize trash collection, recycling, and waste disposal.

   o **How It Works**: **Smart bins** equipped with sensors track the level of waste inside them and send real-time data to waste management systems. When the bins are full, the system automatically schedules pickups, ensuring that trash is collected on time and that resources are used efficiently. AI can also be used to optimize waste routes, reducing fuel consumption and emissions from garbage trucks.

   o **Benefits**: Smart waste management systems reduce the environmental impact of waste collection, improve sanitation, and create cleaner cities. They also help cities save money by optimizing collection schedules, reducing operational costs, and improving recycling rates.

   o **Real-World Example**: **New York City** has adopted a smart waste management system that uses **sensor-equipped trash bins** to monitor waste levels and send alerts when they are full. The system allows the city to optimize trash collection routes, reducing fuel consumption and congestion in busy urban areas. In addition, **Seoul** has implemented an advanced waste tracking system that uses RFID technology to monitor waste disposal and encourage recycling, rewarding residents who properly dispose of recyclable materials.

4. **Autonomous Public Transport**

   o **Overview**: Autonomous vehicles are poised to revolutionize public transport systems in smart cities by reducing congestion, improving safety, and providing more efficient, on-demand services. Self-driving buses, trains, and shuttles will help create an interconnected and automated urban transport network.

   o **How It Works**: Autonomous vehicles use a combination of AI, sensors, and GPS to navigate streets, detect obstacles, and make real-time decisions. These vehicles can be integrated into city transportation networks, providing reliable, efficient, and environmentally friendly alternatives to traditional modes of transport.

   o **Benefits**: Autonomous public transport reduces the need for human drivers, lowers operating

151

costs, and enhances the efficiency of public transportation systems. It can also provide more flexible services, such as on-demand rides, that improve accessibility and reduce traffic congestion.

- o **Real-World Example**: **Dubai** has been testing autonomous vehicles for public transport as part of its Smart City initiative. The city plans to have autonomous taxis and buses on the road by 2030, aiming to reduce traffic congestion and enhance mobility for its residents. In addition, **San Francisco** has been running autonomous shuttle services in certain areas, allowing people to travel without a human driver while gathering data to improve autonomous vehicle technology.

Smart cities are becoming more connected and efficient through the integration of automation technologies in various aspects of urban life. **Automated traffic management**, **smart utilities**, and **waste management systems** are just a few examples of how automation is transforming cities into more sustainable, efficient, and livable environments. Cities like **Singapore**, **Barcelona**, and **Dubai** are leading the way in adopting these technologies, showing the potential for smarter urban development in the future. As automation continues to advance, smart cities will become even more interconnected, offering residents a higher quality of life while reducing environmental impact and improving operational efficiency.

CHAPTER 20

ROBOTICS IN SPACE EXPLORATION: AUTOMATING THE FINAL FRONTIER

How Robots Are Being Used in Space Missions

Robotics plays a crucial role in space exploration by performing tasks that would be dangerous, difficult, or impossible for humans to carry out directly. From exploring distant planets to repairing satellites, robots are used extensively to gather data, conduct experiments, and perform maintenance in the harsh and inhospitable environment of space. By utilizing advanced robotics, space agencies can extend their reach and capabilities, allowing for more ambitious missions and more detailed exploration of outer space.

Key roles of robots in space exploration include:

1. **Surface Exploration**: Robots can explore the surfaces of planets and moons, gathering valuable data about the environment, soil, atmosphere, and potential for life. This includes missions to Mars, Venus, and beyond.

154

2. **Spacecraft Maintenance and Repair**: Robots can be used for routine maintenance, repairs, and upgrades of spacecraft or satellites that are too far from Earth to be serviced by humans.

3. **Sample Collection and Analysis**: Robotic systems are often equipped with tools to collect soil, rock, and atmospheric samples, which are then analyzed for signs of life or to understand the composition of celestial bodies.

4. **Autonomous Operations**: Given the distance and communication delays in space, robots must often operate autonomously, making decisions without direct input from Earth-based controllers.

Robots and autonomous systems are essential to the continued exploration of space, enabling missions that would otherwise be too complex or risky for human astronauts to undertake directly.

Case Studies: Mars Rovers, Autonomous Satellites

1. **Mars Rovers: Exploring the Red Planet**
   o **Overview**: Mars rovers are robotic vehicles designed to explore the surface of Mars, conduct scientific experiments, and send valuable data back to Earth. These rovers are equipped with cameras, sensors, and specialized instruments to

analyze the Martian environment and gather information about the planet's geology, climate, and potential for past or present life.

- o **How It Works**: Mars rovers are equipped with a range of tools, including cameras for taking images, spectrometers for analyzing soil and rock, and robotic arms for collecting samples. The rovers are remotely controlled by mission teams on Earth, but they also have autonomous capabilities that allow them to navigate the surface, avoid obstacles, and carry out certain tasks without direct human intervention.

- o **Real-World Example**: **Curiosity Rover**: Launched by NASA in 2011, the **Curiosity rover** is one of the most successful and well-known Mars rovers. It is equipped with a variety of scientific instruments that have allowed it to explore Gale Crater and conduct a detailed analysis of Martian soil and rocks. Curiosity's ability to analyze the chemical composition of rocks and soil has helped scientists confirm the presence of ancient water on Mars, a key discovery in the search for signs of past life.

- o **Another Example**: **Perseverance Rover**: Launched in 2020, NASA's **Perseverance rover** is equipped with more advanced technology than its predecessors. It carries instruments like the **MOXIE** experiment, designed to convert carbon dioxide into oxygen, as well as a drill for collecting core samples. Perseverance is also the first rover to attempt a controlled flight on another planet, with its **Ingenuity helicopter** taking multiple successful flights over Mars' surface, demonstrating the potential for aerial exploration in future missions.

2. **Autonomous Satellites: Revolutionizing Space Infrastructure**

   o **Overview**: Autonomous satellites are spacecraft equipped with robotic systems designed to carry out tasks such as monitoring, communication, maintenance, and even repairs while in orbit. These satellites often operate autonomously to avoid delays caused by communication issues and long transmission times between Earth and space.

   o **How It Works**: Autonomous satellites are equipped with AI and sensors that allow them to assess their environment, adjust their orbits, and perform maintenance tasks without human input. They can also detect and avoid potential threats, like space debris or other objects, using real-time data.

157

- o **Real-World Example**: **Astroscale**: A private company, **Astroscale**, is developing autonomous satellite technology for satellite debris removal. Their **ELSA-d (End-of-Life Services by Astroscale Demonstration)** mission is designed to capture and remove defunct satellites from orbit, a critical task as space becomes increasingly congested with debris. The autonomous system uses a robotic arm to latch onto and deorbit old satellites, preventing potential collisions with operational satellites.

- o **Another Example: NASA's On-Orbit Servicing, Assembly, and Manufacturing (OSAM)**: NASA's **OSAM** program is working to develop autonomous satellite technology that can repair, refuel, and upgrade satellites in space. These autonomous satellites are designed to extend the operational life of satellites, saving costs on launching new ones and ensuring more sustainable use of space resources. The **OSAM-1** mission, scheduled for the near future, will demonstrate the capability of robotic servicing on orbit.

3. **Robotic Arms: Spacecraft Maintenance and Satellite Repair**

- ○ **Overview**: Robotic arms are frequently used in space for tasks such as assembling spacecraft, repairing satellites, and conducting scientific experiments. These arms are often mounted on space stations or spacecraft, enabling robots to perform intricate tasks in space that would otherwise require human involvement.

- ○ **How It Works**: Robotic arms on spacecraft and space stations are controlled remotely by astronauts or mission operators on Earth. Some systems, such as the **Canadarm** used on the **International Space Station (ISS)**, are designed for high-precision tasks, including attaching modules, deploying satellites, and repairing external components of the ISS. These robotic arms are equipped with advanced sensors and AI capabilities, enabling them to perform delicate operations in zero gravity.

- ○ **Real-World Example: Canadarm2**: Canadarm2 is a Canadian-designed robotic arm mounted on the ISS. It plays a critical role in maintaining and operating the station, including moving cargo, performing spacewalks, and capturing incoming spacecraft for docking. The arm is controlled by astronauts aboard the ISS or remotely by mission control, and it can also perform autonomous operations, such as detecting and avoiding obstacles.

4. **Space Robotic Mining and Exploration**

o **Overview**: Robotic systems are being developed for future space exploration missions to harvest resources from celestial bodies such as the Moon, Mars, and asteroids. These robotic miners will be capable of extracting valuable materials, such as water and metals, that could be used to support future human settlements in space.

o **How It Works**: Robotic mining systems are designed to operate autonomously on the surface of planets or asteroids, collecting resources and sending them back to Earth or to orbiting spacecraft. These robots use a variety of tools, including drills, scoops, and extractors, to dig into the surface and collect samples.

o **Real-World Example**: **NASA's Resource Prospector**: NASA has been working on the **Resource Prospector mission**, which aims to send a robotic rover to the Moon to identify and mine resources, particularly water ice, which could be used for fuel or drinking water. The rover is designed to autonomously collect samples and analyze them on-site, enabling

160

future space missions to make use of local resources.

Robots are playing an increasingly essential role in **space exploration**, allowing scientists and engineers to explore distant planets, repair satellites, and even mine resources from celestial bodies. From **Mars rovers** like **Curiosity** and **Perseverance** to **autonomous satellites** and **robotic arms** on the **ISS**, robots are extending humanity's reach in space and enabling missions that were once thought to be impossible. As technology continues to advance, robots will become even more integral to the future of space exploration, opening up new possibilities for scientific discovery and resource utilization in the final frontier.

CHAPTER 21

AUTONOMOUS DRONES: THE SKY'S THE LIMIT

The Rise of Drones in Various Industries

Drones, also known as **unmanned aerial vehicles (UAVs)**, have seen a remarkable rise in popularity across various industries in recent years. Once primarily used by the military for reconnaissance, drones are now being utilized for a wide array of commercial applications, revolutionizing industries ranging from delivery to agriculture to surveillance.

The rise of **autonomous drones**, which can operate without human intervention, has taken this technology to new heights. Thanks to advancements in AI, GPS technology, and machine learning, drones can now navigate complex environments, make real-time decisions, and carry out tasks with minimal human oversight. These capabilities have made drones a game-changer in industries where speed, precision, and cost-efficiency are critical.

Key drivers of the drone revolution include:

1. **Cost-Effectiveness**: Drones can reduce the need for manned aircraft and ground vehicles, cutting operational costs.

2. **Speed and Efficiency**: Drones can access hard-to-reach areas quickly and perform tasks much faster than traditional methods.

3. **Precision**: With sensors, cameras, and GPS, drones can deliver high levels of accuracy, especially in tasks like surveying or spraying crops.

4. **Safety**: Drones are increasingly being used in dangerous environments, where human presence would be risky, such as in disaster zones, hazardous waste sites, or high-altitude locations.

Applications: Delivery, Surveillance, Agriculture, and More

1. **Drone Delivery**

    o **Overview**: One of the most talked-about applications of drones is **delivery**. Companies are using drones to transport goods quickly and efficiently, especially in areas where traditional delivery methods are slower or more costly.

    o **How It Works**: Drones for delivery typically carry small packages and navigate autonomously using GPS and sensors. Delivery drones can take off, land, and fly to a designated location, often avoiding traffic and congestion on the ground.

These drones can carry packages ranging from food and medicine to small electronics and personal goods.

o **Benefits**: Drone delivery offers faster service, reduces delivery costs, and helps avoid the inefficiencies of traffic. This technology is particularly valuable for last-mile delivery, the final stage of getting a product from a warehouse to a customer's door.

o **Real-World Example**: **Amazon Prime Air** has been testing autonomous drones for delivery, aiming to make package delivery as fast as 30 minutes. The drones are designed to carry packages weighing up to five pounds and use advanced sensors to navigate and avoid obstacles. Other companies, like **Wing (Alphabet)** and **UPS**, are also exploring drone delivery services, with some already conducting pilot programs in select cities.

2. **Drone Surveillance and Security**

o **Overview**: Drones have become an invaluable tool for surveillance and security, providing real-time monitoring of large areas, such as cities, borders, and private properties. These drones can be equipped with high-definition cameras, infrared sensors, and other surveillance tools to gather intelligence and enhance security measures.

- o **How It Works**: Surveillance drones are often autonomous, programmed to patrol certain areas or follow specific routes. Equipped with cameras and sensors, they can capture video, monitor crowds, and detect unusual activity. These drones transmit live feeds back to security personnel or AI systems that analyze the data and trigger alerts in case of a threat.

- o **Benefits**: Drones can cover vast areas quickly, providing detailed, real-time monitoring without the need for human security personnel to be present at all times. They can also reach difficult-to-access or dangerous locations, improving safety and security in places where human surveillance would be impractical.

- o **Real-World Example**: **Dubai Police** has launched **autonomous drones** for patrolling certain areas in the city. These drones are equipped with cameras and facial recognition technology to monitor and identify suspects in real-time. In addition, **the U.S. Department of Homeland Security** has employed drones for border surveillance, using them to monitor vast stretches of land and detect unauthorized crossings.

3. **Drones in Agriculture**

  o **Overview**: Drones are playing an increasingly important role in **precision agriculture** by providing farmers with real-time data on crop health, soil conditions, and overall field performance. By collecting aerial imagery and sensor data, drones help farmers make better decisions about irrigation, fertilization, and pest control.

  o **How It Works**: Agricultural drones are typically equipped with **multispectral** and **thermal cameras** to capture high-resolution images of crops. These images help farmers identify areas of the field that require attention, such as areas with water stress, pest infestations, or nutrient deficiencies. Drones can also be used to spray pesticides or fertilizers directly onto crops with pinpoint accuracy, reducing the use of chemicals and minimizing environmental impact.

  o **Benefits**: Drones increase efficiency, reduce labor costs, and help improve crop yields by allowing for more precise application of water, fertilizers, and pesticides. They also enable farmers to monitor large fields quickly and make data-driven decisions that improve sustainability and crop quality.

- o **Real-World Example**: **DJI** is one of the leaders in agricultural drone technology, offering drones that are used by farmers around the world to monitor and manage crops. In Japan, **XAG** has developed drones that autonomously fly over fields to spray pesticides, fertilizers, and herbicides, reducing the need for manual labor and ensuring more accurate application of chemicals.

4. **Disaster Response and Search-and-Rescue**

- o **Overview**: Drones have become an essential tool for **disaster response** and **search-and-rescue operations**. When natural disasters such as earthquakes, floods, or hurricanes occur, drones are used to assess damage, locate survivors, and deliver supplies to inaccessible areas.

- o **How It Works**: Equipped with high-resolution cameras, infrared sensors, and GPS, drones can fly over disaster zones, providing emergency responders with real-time images and maps. They can also locate survivors by identifying heat signatures or using AI to detect human movement in debris.

- o **Benefits**: Drones reduce the time it takes to assess damage and locate survivors, enabling faster response times and more efficient use of resources. They can access areas that are dangerous or difficult for humans to reach, such as collapsed buildings or areas with hazardous conditions.

- o **Real-World Example**: After the **2015 Nepal earthquake**, drones were used to quickly survey the damage and create 3D maps of the affected areas. The data collected by drones was used to plan rescue missions and deliver supplies to hard-to-reach areas. Similarly, **the Red Cross** and other humanitarian organizations have used drones in disaster areas to deliver medical supplies, food, and water to those in need.

5. **Environmental Monitoring and Conservation**

- o **Overview**: Drones are increasingly being used for environmental monitoring and conservation efforts. They can be deployed to monitor ecosystems, track wildlife, and collect data on environmental changes, such as deforestation, water quality, and climate change.

- o **How It Works**: Drones equipped with sensors, cameras, and other monitoring tools can fly over forests, rivers, oceans, and wildlife habitats, gathering data on environmental conditions. This data is then analyzed to track trends, detect environmental threats, and inform conservation strategies.

- o **Benefits**: Drones provide a cost-effective and non-invasive way to monitor large areas, improving the ability to track environmental changes and protect ecosystems. They can also help researchers access difficult-to-reach habitats, such as the tops of trees or the deep ocean.

- o **Real-World Example**: **Conservation drones** are being used in places like the **Amazon Rainforest** to monitor deforestation. These drones collect data on the state of the forest, identify illegal logging activities, and help authorities enforce conservation laws. In addition, **ocean conservationists** are using drones to track sea turtle nests and monitor marine ecosystems.

The rise of **autonomous drones** is transforming industries by enabling faster, safer, and more efficient operations across various sectors. Whether it's **drone delivery**, **surveillance**, **agriculture**, or **disaster response**, these

169

versatile machines are revolutionizing how tasks are performed and how industries operate. Drones are no longer just a novelty; they are essential tools that are shaping the future of transportation, security, agriculture, and conservation. As technology continues to evolve, the potential applications for autonomous drones are virtually limitless, making them an invaluable asset in modern society.

CHAPTER 22

AI IN CUSTOMER SERVICE: CHATBOTS, VIRTUAL ASSISTANTS, AND BEYOND

How AI is Transforming Customer Support

Artificial Intelligence (AI) is fundamentally transforming the way businesses interact with their customers, especially in the realm of customer support. By utilizing technologies such as **machine learning**, **natural language processing (NLP)**, and **speech recognition**, AI enables companies to deliver more efficient, personalized, and accessible customer service. AI-driven customer service solutions, such as **chatbots** and **virtual assistants**, are now commonplace in industries ranging from **banking** to **retail**, providing businesses with tools to engage customers and resolve issues more effectively.

AI in customer service offers several benefits:

1. **24/7 Availability**: AI systems, such as chatbots and virtual assistants, can work around the clock, providing instant support to customers regardless of time zones.

171

2. **Cost Reduction**: By automating routine tasks and answering common customer queries, AI reduces the need for large call centers and human agents, allowing businesses to cut operational costs.

3. **Personalization**: AI can analyze customer data and previous interactions to provide personalized service, such as recommending products or offering tailored solutions.

4. **Efficiency and Speed**: AI systems can quickly process and analyze large volumes of customer queries, providing faster responses and reducing wait times for customers.

5. **Scalability**: AI solutions can handle thousands of interactions simultaneously, making it easier for businesses to scale their customer service operations without sacrificing quality.

As AI continues to evolve, its role in customer service is expected to expand further, enhancing both the customer experience and business outcomes.

Examples: Chatbots in Banking, Virtual Assistants in Retail

1. **Chatbots in Banking**
   o **Overview**: The banking industry has embraced AI-powered **chatbots** to handle a wide range of customer service functions,

from checking account balances to answering queries about loans or credit card applications. By automating these interactions, banks are able to provide faster service and reduce the workload on human customer support agents.

- **How It Works**: Bank chatbots use **natural language processing (NLP)** to understand and interpret customer inquiries. Customers can interact with the chatbot through text or voice, and the AI system responds with accurate, contextually relevant information. For more complex queries, the chatbot can escalate the issue to a human agent.

- **Benefits**: Chatbots in banking help improve efficiency by quickly answering routine questions, such as balance inquiries, transaction histories, or the status of loan applications. This allows human agents to focus on more complicated or sensitive customer needs. Additionally, chatbots can provide 24/7 customer support, ensuring that customers can get help at any time.

173

- o **Real-World Example**: **Bank of America's Erica**: Erica is a virtual assistant powered by AI that helps customers with a variety of tasks, such as checking balances, paying bills, and offering personalized financial advice. Erica can respond to voice and text commands, making it easy for customers to interact with their accounts. In 2020, Bank of America reported that Erica helped save time for customers by completing over **200 million customer requests**.

- o **Another Example**: **Capital One's Eno**: Eno is a chatbot developed by **Capital One** to handle customer queries and assist with everyday banking tasks. Eno can help customers track spending, receive account alerts, and even answer questions about transactions. Its advanced NLP capabilities allow customers to interact with the chatbot in a natural and conversational way, improving the customer experience.

2. **Virtual Assistants in Retail**

- o **Overview**: Virtual assistants powered by AI are increasingly being used in **retail** to

174

provide customer support, answer product-related questions, and assist with the purchasing process. Virtual assistants help guide customers through their shopping journey, offering personalized recommendations, addressing concerns, and simplifying the buying process.

o **How It Works**: Virtual assistants in retail typically use **AI algorithms** to analyze customer preferences, purchasing history, and behavior. They can provide product recommendations, assist with checkout, and even track the status of orders. Some virtual assistants are also integrated with voice recognition technology, enabling customers to interact with them via voice commands.

o **Benefits**: Virtual assistants in retail improve customer engagement by offering personalized recommendations based on previous purchases or browsing habits. They also reduce friction during the purchasing process by answering customer questions in real-time, streamlining the shopping experience.

o **Real-World Example**: **Amazon Alexa in Retail**: **Amazon** has integrated AI-powered virtual assistants into its **Alexa** platform, allowing customers to make purchases, track shipments, and ask for product recommendations simply by using voice commands. This hands-free experience enhances convenience and improves the shopping experience, particularly for customers who may want to shop while multitasking. Retailers can also integrate Alexa into their own e-commerce platforms to offer a seamless voice shopping experience.

o **Another Example**: **Sephora's Virtual Assistant**: **Sephora**, a leading beauty retailer, offers a **virtual assistant** on its mobile app that helps customers find products, track orders, and receive personalized beauty advice. The assistant uses AI to suggest makeup and skincare products based on customer preferences, skin types, and previous purchases. This AI-driven service enhances the customer experience by providing tailored recommendations and reducing decision fatigue when shopping for beauty products.

3. **AI-Powered Customer Support in E-commerce**

   o **Overview**: AI-powered customer support is becoming increasingly common in **e-commerce**, where chatbots and virtual assistants are used to handle customer inquiries, track orders, and assist with returns or refunds. These AI systems can automate many aspects of the customer service process, allowing businesses to respond faster and handle more inquiries at once.

   o **How It Works**: E-commerce platforms integrate chatbots or virtual assistants into their websites or apps, allowing customers to quickly ask questions and receive real-time answers. These systems can handle a wide range of queries, from product availability to shipping details, and can escalate more complex issues to human agents when necessary. Many AI systems are also integrated with CRM (Customer Relationship Management) software, enabling them to access a customer's order history and provide personalized support.

   o **Benefits**: AI customer support in e-commerce helps businesses scale their operations without compromising on service quality. It allows companies to handle high volumes of customer inquiries during peak shopping times, such as during sales events or holidays, while providing customers with faster, more accurate responses.

- o **Real-World Example: H&M's Chatbot: H&M** launched an AI-powered chatbot on its website that helps customers find products, check availability, and receive style recommendations. The chatbot uses **machine learning** to understand customer preferences and improve its suggestions over time, offering a personalized shopping experience for users. This virtual assistant enhances the overall shopping experience by providing quick answers and product recommendations.

4. **AI and Customer Insights**

    - o **Overview**: AI is not only used to assist with customer support tasks, but also to analyze customer behavior and gain insights into preferences, trends, and sentiment. By analyzing large volumes of customer data, AI systems can identify patterns and predict future behavior, helping businesses tailor their marketing, sales, and customer service strategies.

- o **How It Works**: AI systems process customer data from various touchpoints, such as emails, social media interactions, and previous purchases. This data is then analyzed to uncover insights into customer needs, sentiment, and buying habits. Businesses can use this information to improve their product offerings, design targeted marketing campaigns, and anticipate customer concerns or needs.

- o **Benefits**: By using AI to analyze customer data, businesses can improve their understanding of their customers, enabling them to offer more personalized services and products. AI-driven insights also allow companies to address potential issues proactively, improving customer satisfaction and loyalty.

- o **Real-World Example: Spotify's Recommendation Algorithm**: **Spotify** uses AI to analyze users' listening habits and provide personalized playlists, song recommendations, and new releases based on their preferences. The AI system continually learns from user interactions, refining its suggestions and improving the user experience. This personalized approach has helped Spotify maintain its position as one of the leading music streaming platforms globally.

AI in customer service is transforming the way businesses interact with their customers, providing faster, more personalized, and scalable solutions. **Chatbots** in banking and **virtual assistants** in retail are just the beginning of how AI can streamline customer support, from answering simple queries to providing tailored recommendations. As AI continues to evolve, businesses will be able to offer even more intuitive and efficient services, further enhancing customer satisfaction and loyalty. With the ability to operate 24/7, provide personalized support, and analyze vast amounts of data, AI is revolutionizing the customer service landscape across industries.

CHAPTER 23

THE LEGAL FRAMEWORK FOR AUTOMATION: REGULATION AND COMPLIANCE

The Current State of Laws Surrounding Automation and Robots

As automation technologies continue to evolve and integrate into various sectors, including manufacturing, transportation, healthcare, and customer service, the legal framework surrounding automation is becoming increasingly complex. Many of the technologies driving automation, such as robots, artificial intelligence (AI), and autonomous systems, often outpace existing laws and regulations, creating gaps and uncertainties in legal oversight.

The legal landscape for automation and robots is still developing, and many jurisdictions are grappling with how to regulate these technologies. However, certain foundational principles are emerging to address key concerns related to safety, liability, and intellectual property, among others.

Key areas where laws are currently focused include:

1. **Liability and Accountability**: When robots or automated systems cause harm—whether through accidents, malfunctions, or unethical decisions—who is responsible? This question is particularly relevant in the context of autonomous vehicles, medical robots, and AI-driven systems.

2. **Data Privacy and Security**: Automation technologies often rely on the collection and processing of large amounts of data. Data privacy laws, such as the **General Data Protection Regulation (GDPR)** in the EU, govern how personal data should be handled and safeguarded.

3. **Intellectual Property**: As robots and AI systems become more innovative, questions of intellectual property rights—such as patents, copyrights, and ownership—are increasingly important. For instance, who owns the intellectual property generated by an AI system or autonomous robot: the creator of the algorithm, the company deploying the robot, or the machine itself?

4. **Workplace Safety and Employment Laws**: Automation often involves the displacement of workers or a significant shift in labor practices. In response, laws around workplace safety, unemployment insurance, and worker rights are evolving to account for the integration of robots and automation into workspaces.

182

5. **Ethics and Regulation of AI**: As AI systems become more capable of making decisions, ethical concerns regarding their use are at the forefront. Issues such as **bias in AI algorithms**, the **transparency of decision-making processes**, and the potential for **autonomous robots** to act unpredictably are critical areas of focus for regulators.

In many countries, national and international organizations are working to develop frameworks and guidelines to address these challenges and ensure that automation technologies are developed and deployed responsibly.

Challenges in Regulating Emerging Technologies like Autonomous Vehicles

One of the most significant challenges in regulating automation is the development of **autonomous vehicles (AVs)**. Self-driving cars, trucks, and drones present unique regulatory hurdles due to their complexity and potential for widespread societal impact. These vehicles rely on AI, machine learning, and real-time data to make decisions on the road, and this raises a variety of legal and ethical issues that governments and industries are still grappling with.

1. **Safety and Standards**

- o **Challenge**: Ensuring the safety of autonomous vehicles is paramount, especially as these systems must interact with human-driven vehicles and pedestrians. Current safety regulations for vehicles were not designed with self-driving cars in mind, which means new standards must be created to address the unique risks posed by AVs.

- o **How It Works**: Various regulatory bodies are working to define safety standards for AVs. For example, the **National Highway Traffic Safety Administration (NHTSA)** in the U.S. has developed guidelines for testing autonomous vehicles but lacks specific safety regulations tailored to fully autonomous systems.

- o **Real-World Example**: In 2018, **Uber**'s self-driving car was involved in a fatal accident with a pedestrian in Arizona, leading to widespread concerns about the safety of autonomous vehicles. This incident highlighted the need for clearer and stricter safety regulations to ensure that AVs can operate safely and ethically on public roads.

2. **Liability and Insurance**

- o **Challenge**: When an autonomous vehicle is involved in an accident, who is responsible for the damages? Is it the manufacturer of the vehicle, the developer of the AI software, or the owner of the vehicle? These questions are difficult to answer under current laws, which are generally designed for human drivers.

- o **How It Works**: Regulators are working on frameworks for determining liability in AV-related accidents. Some suggestions include holding manufacturers responsible for system failures or accidents caused by their vehicles, while others propose creating a new category of insurance specifically for AVs. Autonomous vehicles also require new models for **vehicle liability insurance**, where the legal responsibility may shift from the driver to the developer or manufacturer.

- o **Real-World Example**: **Waymo**, Google's self-driving car project, has faced legal challenges related to liability after incidents involving its autonomous vehicles. In 2018, a lawsuit was filed against **Waymo** after one of its cars was involved in a collision with a human-driven vehicle. As AV technology continues to evolve, legal frameworks will need to address these complex liability questions.

3. **Ethical and Moral Decision-Making**

185

o **Challenge**: Autonomous vehicles, especially self-driving cars, may encounter situations that require ethical decision-making. For instance, if an AV has to choose between swerving to avoid hitting a pedestrian but causing harm to the passenger, what should it do? These types of moral dilemmas raise important questions about how AI should be programmed to make decisions in such scenarios.

o **How It Works**: There is no consensus on how autonomous vehicles should handle moral dilemmas. Ethical decision-making in AVs is a topic of intense debate among policymakers, ethicists, and AI researchers. Some argue that ethical frameworks should be standardized, while others believe these decisions should be left to individual developers or society at large.

o **Real-World Example**: In 2016, **Tesla's Autopilot** feature was involved in an accident that raised questions about the ethical implications of self-driving technology. The vehicle's AI system was unable to recognize an obstacle in its path, which resulted in a fatal crash. This highlighted the need for regulations that consider the ethical implications of automated decision-making.

4. **Regulatory Fragmentation**

   o **Challenge**: Another key issue in regulating autonomous vehicles is the **fragmentation** of regulations across different regions and countries. While some countries, like **Germany** and **Singapore**, have already begun to create regulations for AV testing and deployment, others are still lagging behind.

   o **How It Works**: The lack of uniformity in regulations makes it difficult for companies to deploy autonomous vehicles on a global scale. Companies like **Tesla**, **Waymo**, and **Uber** are faced with navigating multiple regulatory frameworks that vary from country to country and even from state to state within the U.S.

   o **Real-World Example**: In **Europe**, countries like **Germany** have introduced laws specifically for testing autonomous vehicles, while other countries in the EU have yet to establish clear guidelines. This regulatory inconsistency poses challenges for companies looking to develop AVs and deploy them globally.

The regulation of **autonomous vehicles** and **automation technologies** presents numerous challenges related to safety, liability, ethics, and legal consistency. Governments and industries around the world are working to create frameworks that ensure these technologies are deployed responsibly and safely. The legal landscape is still evolving, and as technologies like autonomous vehicles, drones, and AI continue to advance, regulations must adapt to address new risks and opportunities. Addressing these challenges will require collaboration between regulators, companies, and the public to ensure that automation technologies benefit society as a whole while minimizing potential harm.

CHAPTER 24

AUTOMATION AND CYBERSECURITY: PROTECTING SMART MACHINES FROM THREATS

The Risks Associated with Automated Systems and the Need for Cybersecurity

As automation technologies become more integrated into everyday life, from autonomous vehicles to smart homes, the **cybersecurity** risks associated with these systems also increase. Automated systems, such as robots, drones, and AI-driven devices, often rely on **network connectivity**, **cloud computing**, and **data-sharing** to perform tasks efficiently. While these technologies offer significant benefits in terms of convenience and efficiency, they also create potential vulnerabilities that can be exploited by cybercriminals.

The rise of **smart machines** and **connected devices** means that automation systems are increasingly exposed to cyberattacks. These risks can range from data breaches to system hijacking, and in some cases, they can result in physical harm, financial loss, or reputational damage. Given the rapid adoption of automation technologies, the importance of securing these systems cannot be overstated.

Key risks associated with automated systems include:

1. **Data Vulnerabilities**: Automated systems often rely on vast amounts of sensitive data, which can be targeted by cyberattacks. For example, AI systems may process personal data, financial information, or medical records, all of which are valuable targets for cybercriminals.

2. **IoT Security**: **Internet of Things (IoT)** devices, such as smart home appliances, connected cars, and wearable devices, are often vulnerable to attacks due to weak or poorly implemented security protocols. These devices can serve as entry points for cybercriminals to access larger, more sensitive networks.

3. **Autonomous System Hijacking**: In the case of autonomous vehicles, drones, or robots, a hacker could potentially take control of the system, causing it to malfunction or behave unpredictably. This could lead to physical damage or a threat to human safety.

4. **Malware and Ransomware**: Just like traditional IT systems, automated systems are susceptible to malware, ransomware, and viruses. These can be used to disrupt

operations, steal data, or extort money from organizations.

As automation technologies continue to expand, it becomes critical to implement robust cybersecurity strategies to protect smart machines and ensure their safe and ethical use.

Real-World Examples: Cyberattacks on Smart Devices, Drones

1. **Cyberattacks on Smart Devices**
   - **Overview**: **Smart devices** in homes and businesses—such as smart thermostats, cameras, refrigerators, and lighting systems—are increasingly connected to the internet. However, many of these devices lack strong security features, making them vulnerable to cyberattacks.
   - **How It Works**: Smart devices can be compromised through weak passwords, unpatched vulnerabilities, or insecure communication channels. Once a device is hacked, attackers can gain control over it, use it to launch attacks on other systems, or collect sensitive data.
   - **Real-World Example**: **The Mirai Botnet**: In 2016, a large-scale cyberattack known as the **Mirai Botnet** exploited vulnerabilities in unsecured IoT devices, including cameras and

routers. The botnet took control of these devices and used them to launch a **Distributed Denial-of-Service (DDoS)** attack on major websites, including **Twitter**, **Netflix**, and **Spotify**. This attack demonstrated the vulnerability of smart devices and the need for stronger security protocols in IoT networks.

- o **Another Example: Ring Doorbell Hacking**: In 2019, several incidents were reported where hackers gained access to users' **Ring doorbell cameras**. By exploiting weak passwords and security flaws, the attackers were able to remotely view live video feeds and even communicate with residents through the device's two-way audio feature. This highlighted the risks associated with smart home devices and the importance of securing them with strong, unique passwords and encryption.

2. **Cyberattacks on Drones**

- o **Overview**: **Drones**, particularly those used in commercial applications, such as delivery, surveillance, or infrastructure inspection, are highly vulnerable to cyberattacks. Drones are often connected to remote control systems, GPS, and cloud services, making them susceptible to hacking, spoofing, or hijacking.

- How It Works: Drones can be attacked in several ways, including jamming their GPS signals, intercepting communication between the drone and its operator, or taking control of the drone remotely. These attacks can cause the drone to crash, behave erratically, or even be used for malicious purposes, such as spying or delivering contraband.

- **Real-World Example: UK Drone Attack at Gatwick Airport**: In December 2018, **Gatwick Airport** in London was forced to shut down its operations for several days due to a series of **drone sightings** near the airport. Authorities suspected the drones were intentionally flown into restricted airspace, potentially as part of a coordinated cyberattack aimed at disrupting operations. Although the perpetrators were not immediately caught, the incident exposed the vulnerability of drones in critical infrastructure environments and raised concerns about the lack of robust cybersecurity measures to protect against such attacks.

- **Another Example: DJI Drones Hacked**: In 2017, a report surfaced that the popular **DJI** drones had security vulnerabilities that could allow hackers to take control of the drones. The vulnerabilities were linked to the software used to control the drones and could allow hackers to intercept and manipulate flight data or even take over the drone's navigation systems. DJI responded by introducing stronger security protocols, but the incident highlighted the potential for cyberattacks on drones, especially when deployed for sensitive missions, such as surveillance or military operations.

3. **Autonomous Vehicle Cyberattacks**

- o **Overview**: **Autonomous vehicles** (AVs), which rely on AI, sensors, and GPS for navigation, are becoming increasingly prevalent. However, these systems are highly susceptible to cyberattacks, as a hacker could potentially gain control of a vehicle's functions, leading to significant safety risks.

- o **How It Works**: Autonomous vehicles communicate with external systems, such as GPS, traffic monitoring systems, and other vehicles, which creates potential entry points for hackers. By intercepting or spoofing signals, or exploiting software vulnerabilities, attackers could manipulate the vehicle's behavior, causing it to malfunction, veer off course, or even crash.

- o **Real-World Example**: Jeep Cherokee Hack: In 2015, researchers demonstrated the ability to remotely hack into a **Jeep Cherokee** while it was driving. By exploiting vulnerabilities in the vehicle's infotainment system, they gained control over critical functions, such as steering, braking, and acceleration. The incident revealed the potential risks posed by connected vehicles and the need for stronger cybersecurity measures in autonomous cars.

- o **Another Example**: Tesla Model S Hack: In 2016, a team of Chinese researchers was able to hack into a **Tesla Model S** by exploiting vulnerabilities in the vehicle's software. They were able to remotely control the car's door locks, navigation, and climate controls, demonstrating that even high-end, widely used autonomous vehicles could be vulnerable to cyberattacks.

4. **Robotic Systems in Industrial Control**

- o **Overview**: Industrial robots, used in manufacturing and automation processes, are another area of concern when it comes to cybersecurity. These robots often communicate with central control systems and are linked to networks that may not be adequately protected from cyber threats.

195

- o **How It Works**: Cybercriminals can exploit vulnerabilities in a factory's network to gain access to robotic systems. Once inside the network, attackers can manipulate the robots' behavior, causing disruptions in the production process, compromising safety protocols, or even causing physical damage to machinery.

- o **Real-World Example: Stuxnet Worm**: In 2010, the **Stuxnet** worm was used to target and disable **Iran's nuclear enrichment facilities**. Although not specifically aimed at robots, the attack demonstrated the vulnerability of industrial control systems. The worm was able to infiltrate the systems controlling the centrifuges, causing them to malfunction. This incident highlighted the importance of securing industrial automation systems and robots that are part of critical infrastructure.

The rise of **automated systems** and **smart machines** has introduced new challenges in **cybersecurity**, as the risks associated with these technologies can affect not only business operations but also public safety. From **cyberattacks on smart devices** and **drones** to **hacking**

autonomous vehicles, the need for robust cybersecurity measures is more pressing than ever. Protecting these systems from external threats requires constant vigilance, advanced security protocols, and collaboration between manufacturers, security experts, and regulators. As the automation landscape continues to grow, it is crucial to develop strategies to safeguard these technologies and ensure that they are used safely and ethically.

CHAPTER 25

THE FUTURE OF AUTOMATION: WHERE ARE WE HEADED?

Predictions for the Future of Automation

The future of automation is poised to revolutionize industries and reshape society in ways that were once the domain of science fiction. As technologies continue to evolve, we can expect automation to expand into new areas, drive unprecedented productivity gains, and significantly alter the way we live and work. However, as automation grows, it will also present new challenges, including the need for effective regulation, upskilling of the workforce, and addressing societal impacts like job displacement.

Here are some key predictions for the future of automation:

1. **Widespread Adoption Across Industries**: Automation will continue to permeate all sectors, from manufacturing and agriculture to healthcare and finance. Robots, AI systems, and automated processes will become integral to daily operations, enhancing efficiency, reducing costs, and enabling businesses to meet the growing demands of a global economy.

2. **Increased Use of Autonomous Systems**: We can expect more widespread use of **autonomous vehicles** (including self-driving cars, trucks, and drones) and **autonomous robots** in various industries. These systems will operate independently, reducing human error and increasing safety while allowing for new applications, such as autonomous deliveries, smart cities, and even space exploration.

3. **AI-Driven Decision Making**: The role of AI in automation will continue to expand, with AI systems taking on more decision-making responsibilities across sectors. From **financial analysis** to **supply chain management**, AI will enable faster and more accurate decision-making by analyzing vast amounts of data and predicting future outcomes.

4. **Personalized Automation in Everyday Life**: Automation will increasingly become a part of **personalized experiences**, from AI-powered virtual assistants to smart homes. Automation will anticipate our needs, optimize our schedules, and help us manage our lives more effectively.

5. **Collaboration Between Humans and Machines**: Rather than replacing humans entirely, future automation systems will work alongside humans, enhancing our capabilities. **Cobots** (collaborative robots) will be commonplace, assisting workers in tasks that require

strength, precision, or repetitive effort, while humans will focus on creative, strategic, and decision-making activities.

As automation continues to advance, its impact will be felt across society, with both positive and negative consequences. How we manage this transition will determine whether automation leads to greater opportunities or exacerbates social inequality.

How Emerging Technologies Like Quantum Computing and Blockchain Might Shape Automation

1. **Quantum Computing and Automation**
   - **Overview**: Quantum computing is an emerging technology that harnesses the principles of quantum mechanics to perform computations that would be impossible or take centuries for classical computers to solve. Quantum computers have the potential to revolutionize automation by solving complex problems at unimaginable speeds, enhancing everything from machine learning algorithms to optimization problems.
   - **How It Works**: Quantum computers leverage **qubits**, which can represent multiple states simultaneously, allowing them to perform parallel computations on a massive scale. This

quantum speed-up can significantly enhance the performance of AI algorithms, optimization models, and complex simulations.

- o **Impact on Automation**: Quantum computing could dramatically accelerate the development of more powerful AI systems, enabling them to process and analyze much larger datasets, optimize supply chains in real-time, and solve problems that are currently out of reach. In automation, this could lead to breakthroughs in areas like robotics, logistics, and healthcare, where highly complex decision-making processes are involved.

- o **Real-World Example**: Companies like **IBM** and **Google** are already making strides in quantum computing research. In the future, quantum computing could enable robots to solve highly complex tasks, such as optimizing manufacturing processes on the fly or enabling more efficient routing for autonomous vehicles. Additionally, quantum AI systems could advance medical research, enabling the discovery of new drugs or treatments by rapidly simulating molecular interactions at the quantum level.

2. Blockchain and Automation

- o **Overview**: **Blockchain** is a decentralized, distributed ledger technology that enables secure and transparent transactions without the need for intermediaries like banks or governments. It is most commonly associated with cryptocurrencies like Bitcoin but has far-reaching implications for automation and other sectors due to its ability to provide trust and security in automated systems.

- o **How It Works**: Blockchain operates through a network of computers (called nodes) that validate and record transactions in "blocks," which are linked together in a chain. Each transaction is time-stamped and cryptographically secured, making it nearly impossible to alter the data once recorded. This transparency and security make blockchain ideal for applications where trust is crucial.

- o **Impact on Automation**: Blockchain could play a transformative role in automating processes that require a high level of transparency, security, and accountability. In industries like **supply chain management**, **finance**, and **healthcare**, blockchain can ensure secure and tamper-proof records of transactions, contracts, and interactions between automated systems.

- o **Real-World Example: Supply Chain Automation**: In the supply chain industry, blockchain is being used to track the journey of goods from manufacturer to consumer. This technology ensures that each step of the process is securely recorded, allowing automated systems to verify the authenticity of products, monitor inventory levels, and even automate payments. For instance, **IBM's Food Trust Network** uses blockchain to track the movement of food products from farm to table, ensuring quality and safety. Automation, powered by blockchain, allows for more efficient inventory management, quicker traceability, and better risk management across global supply chains.

- o **Smart Contracts**: In the context of automation, blockchain's **smart contracts** (self-executing contracts with predefined rules) can be used to automate business agreements. For example, when certain conditions are met (e.g., delivery of goods), a smart contract automatically executes the payment or transfer of assets without requiring human intervention. This could reduce administrative costs and eliminate the need for intermediaries.

3. **Integrating Quantum Computing and Blockchain in Automation**

   o **Synergy of Technologies**: Quantum computing and blockchain may not be completely independent technologies. In fact, their convergence could lead to even more powerful automation solutions. Quantum computing could significantly enhance blockchain technology by optimizing consensus algorithms, improving security protocols, and making transactions faster and more efficient.

   o **Quantum-Enhanced Blockchain**: Quantum computers could be used to develop advanced cryptographic techniques for blockchain, making it more secure against attacks from future quantum computers. On the flip side, blockchain can help secure and provide transparency in quantum computing environments, allowing for the trustworthy execution of quantum-based automated systems.

   o **Impact on Automation**: By combining quantum computing's computational power with blockchain's transparency and security, automation could reach unprecedented levels of efficiency and reliability. For instance, in **financial services**, quantum-powered smart contracts could execute highly complex transactions in milliseconds, with all activities securely recorded on a blockchain. In **robotics**, blockchain could securely manage robot-to-robot communication, while quantum computing could allow robots to optimize their decisions and actions in real-time.

The **future of automation** is set to be shaped by powerful emerging technologies like **quantum computing** and **blockchain**, both of which will bring new capabilities to automated systems. Quantum computing will enable faster, more powerful AI and optimization processes, allowing automated systems to solve problems that are currently out of reach. Meanwhile, blockchain will bring security, transparency, and accountability to automated transactions and interactions, ensuring the integrity of systems across industries. Together, these technologies will enable a new generation of automation that is smarter, faster, and more secure than anything we have today. As these technologies evolve, we can expect automation to become even more integrated into our daily lives, reshaping industries and driving further innovation.

CHAPTER 26

LIVING WITH AUTOMATION: HOW SOCIETY IS ADAPTING

Public Perception of Automation and Its Societal Impacts

The rise of automation has sparked both excitement and concern among the public. While many view automation as a gateway to a more efficient, convenient, and technologically advanced future, others are wary of its potential negative consequences, such as job displacement and increased inequality. How society adapts to automation will largely depend on how these perceptions are addressed and how the benefits and risks of automation are balanced.

Key aspects of the public perception of automation include:

1. **Fear of Job Losses**:
   o One of the most common concerns about automation is its potential to replace human workers, especially in low-skill or repetitive jobs. Industries like **manufacturing**, **transportation**, and **customer service** have already seen significant automation, and many workers worry about the future of their employment. There is a

206

real fear that automation will disproportionately affect blue-collar workers, leading to job displacement and income inequality.

- o **Impact on Society**: While automation may eliminate certain jobs, it can also create new roles and industries, especially in fields like AI development, robotics, data science, and cybersecurity. However, the transition between job loss and job creation can be challenging for individuals and communities, requiring careful planning and support from governments and businesses.

2. **Increased Efficiency and Convenience**:

- o On the other hand, many people are enthusiastic about the benefits of automation, particularly in terms of increased productivity, convenience, and improved quality of life. **Autonomous vehicles**, **smart homes**, **AI-powered assistants**, and **robotic surgeries** are just a few examples of how automation can enhance daily living.

- o **Impact on Society**: Automation promises to improve efficiency in various sectors, from transportation to healthcare to manufacturing. For consumers, automation can mean faster service, more personalized experiences, and reduced costs for goods and services. For industries, it can lead to increased profitability, enhanced scalability, and better customer service.

3. **Concerns Over Inequality and Economic Disparities**:

   o While automation has the potential to create significant wealth, it also risks exacerbating economic inequality. High-skilled workers in tech-related fields may benefit from the growth of automation, while low-skilled workers may face job loss or wage stagnation. This growing divide between the **high-tech** and **low-tech** workforce could contribute to further social and economic inequalities.

   o **Impact on Society**: The gap between those who can adapt to technological change and those who cannot could create societal divides. Policymakers will need to address these issues by ensuring that automation benefits are shared more equally and that displaced workers have access to retraining opportunities and social safety nets.

4. **Trust and Ethical Concerns**:

   o Public trust in automation is also a key factor. As machines take on more decision-making roles, there are concerns about how decisions are made, especially in areas like **autonomous driving, AI in healthcare**, and **robotic surveillance**. Ethical questions, such as how AI systems make life-and-death decisions or whether autonomous systems are biased, are central to the conversation around automation.

o **Impact on Society**: Building trust in automation will require transparency in how these systems work and the ethical frameworks that guide their use. Public skepticism about AI and automation could slow adoption unless ethical concerns are addressed through clear guidelines, accountability, and responsible governance.

How Education and Training Are Evolving to Meet the Needs of a Changing Workforce

As automation continues to reshape the workforce, there is a growing need to adapt education and training systems to prepare workers for new roles and skills. Traditional education models, focused primarily on rote learning and manual tasks, are increasingly insufficient in meeting the demands of a highly automated, technology-driven economy.

Key ways education and training are evolving include:

1. **Focus on STEM Education**:

- o **Science, Technology, Engineering, and Mathematics (STEM)** education is becoming more important as automation and AI technologies continue to advance. Schools, universities, and vocational institutions are increasingly focusing on teaching the skills required to develop, manage, and interact with automated systems, such as coding, data analysis, machine learning, and robotics.

- o **Impact on Society**: By promoting STEM education, societies can prepare the next generation of workers for high-tech roles in fields like AI development, cybersecurity, and robotics. This shift will help ensure that the workforce is equipped with the technical skills necessary to thrive in an automated world.

2. **Reskilling and Upskilling Programs**:

- o As automation displaces some jobs, there is a growing emphasis on **reskilling** and **upskilling** programs to help workers transition to new roles. Governments and private companies are investing in programs that teach workers new skills in areas like digital literacy, programming, and data analytics. These initiatives aim to help workers adapt to the changing job market and find new opportunities in the age of automation.

210

o **Impact on Society**: Reskilling initiatives are essential to ensuring that displaced workers can find new employment. Upskilling programs, on the other hand, allow current workers to stay competitive in an evolving job market. A focus on lifelong learning will be key to reducing the risk of long-term unemployment due to automation.

3. **Lifelong Learning and Online Education**:

o The rapid pace of technological change means that workers must continuously adapt their skills to stay relevant. **Lifelong learning** is becoming a central focus in education, with more people turning to online courses, boot camps, and certification programs to develop new skills.

o **Impact on Society**: Online platforms like **Coursera**, **Udemy**, and **edX** are enabling individuals to acquire specialized skills in fields such as data science, AI, and software development without the need for traditional degrees. This democratization of education makes it easier for workers to learn new skills and stay employable in a rapidly changing job market.

o **Real-World Example**: **Amazon's Upskilling Programs**: Amazon has invested heavily in reskilling its employees to meet the demands of an automated workforce. Through its **Amazon Upskilling** programs, the company offers training in areas such as cloud computing, machine learning, and data analysis. These programs help employees move into higher-skilled roles within the company and prepare for a future where automation plays a bigger role in business operations.

4. **Emphasis on Soft Skills**:
   - While technical skills are crucial, there is also an increasing emphasis on **soft skills**—such as **creativity, problem-solving**, and **emotional intelligence**—which cannot easily be replicated by automation. These skills will remain essential in roles that require human interaction, critical thinking, and decision-making.
   - **Impact on Society**: As automation takes over repetitive tasks, workers with strong soft skills will continue to be in demand, particularly in fields like healthcare, education, customer service, and management. Programs that teach emotional intelligence, communication, and leadership will be critical to preparing workers for a future where automation complements, rather than replaces, human abilities.

5. **Collaboration with Industry**:

212

- o There is a growing trend of educational institutions partnering with **industry leaders** to ensure that curricula are aligned with the skills needed in the workforce. These partnerships help provide students with practical, hands-on experience and ensure that training programs meet the demands of the job market.

- o **Impact on Society**: By collaborating with industry, educational institutions can provide students with relevant skills that are directly applicable to current job roles in automation-heavy fields. This alignment between education and industry will help reduce the skills gap and ensure that the workforce is prepared for the future.

Living with automation presents both opportunities and challenges for society. While automation has the potential to improve efficiency, quality of life, and productivity, it also raises concerns about job displacement, inequality, and the ethical use of technology. How society adapts will depend on how well we address these issues, ensuring that the benefits of automation are shared equitably and that workers are prepared for the changes ahead.

213

Education and training are evolving to meet the needs of a changing workforce by focusing on STEM education, reskilling, lifelong learning, and soft skills development. By equipping individuals with the right skills and fostering a culture of continuous learning, societies can ensure that automation leads to greater opportunity rather than greater disparity. As we navigate the future, preparing the workforce for automation will be key to creating a prosperous, inclusive society where technology enhances human potential rather than replacing it.

CHAPTER 27

CONCLUSION: EMBRACING THE FUTURE OF SMART MACHINES

Recap of Automation's Role in Reshaping the World

Over the course of this exploration, we've seen how **automation** is no longer just a trend but a transformative force that is reshaping industries, societies, and daily life. From **autonomous vehicles** and **smart homes** to **robotic systems** in healthcare and **AI-powered customer service**, automation is enabling new efficiencies, improving safety, and creating possibilities that were once unimaginable.

The role of **smart machines** and **robots** in industries such as manufacturing, agriculture, healthcare, finance, and logistics is undeniable. Through the use of **AI, machine learning**, and **robotic systems**, automation is driving productivity, reducing costs, and allowing for more personalized and efficient services. We've seen how automated systems can optimize supply chains, enhance customer experiences, and even aid in disaster response and environmental conservation.

215

Furthermore, automation is not just about replacing humans. It's about complementing human abilities, freeing people from mundane and repetitive tasks, and enabling them to focus on higher-level, creative, and problem-solving roles. This collaboration between **humans and machines** is one of the most promising aspects of the future of automation, as it has the potential to create new job opportunities while improving efficiency and performance in ways we never thought possible.

However, automation also presents challenges. The fears around **job displacement, data privacy,** and **ethical concerns** must be addressed for automation to be successfully integrated into society. Governments, businesses, and individuals need to work together to ensure that these concerns are met with thoughtful regulation, education, and support systems that help society adapt to these changes.

Final Thoughts on the Potential for Automation to Improve Quality of Life

Looking ahead, the potential of automation to improve our **quality of life** is immense. By improving productivity and safety, reducing human error, and enabling smarter, more sustainable practices, automation can contribute to a better, more convenient, and more equitable world.

- **In Healthcare**, robots and AI can help diagnose diseases earlier, assist with surgeries, and provide personalized care to patients. Automation has the potential to reduce human error and improve patient outcomes, leading to a healthier global population.
- **In Agriculture**, automated systems can optimize crop production, conserve resources, and address food security challenges. Precision farming powered by drones and AI can help reduce the environmental footprint of farming while ensuring food is produced efficiently to meet growing demand.
- **In Daily Life**, smart devices and assistants can make our homes more comfortable and efficient, automate household chores, and help us manage our time better, allowing for more leisure and family time.
- **In Transportation**, autonomous vehicles could reduce accidents, decrease traffic congestion, and lower emissions, making our cities safer and more sustainable.

The key to realizing this potential is ensuring that automation serves **human needs**—not just efficiency or profit. It's about creating systems that empower individuals, improve lives, and build a society that is better connected, more inclusive, and more sustainable. The future of automation is not about machines replacing humans, but about machines enhancing human capabilities, solving complex problems, and providing solutions to some of our biggest challenges.

As we continue to embrace **smart machines** and **automation**, we must do so with a balanced approach—one that fosters innovation and progress while considering the ethical, social, and economic implications. If we can achieve this, the future of automation promises a world that is not only more efficient and technologically advanced but also fairer, safer, and more fulfilling for all.

www.ingramcontent.com/pod-product-compliance
Lightning Source LLC
LaVergne TN
LVHW051325050326
832903LV00031B/3369